MAKING
MISSION HAPPEN

Year-Round Program of Education for Mission
in the Local Church and Community

arthur o. f. bauer

Friendship Press • New York

BV
2090
.B38
1974

Library of Congress Cataloging in Publication Data

Bauer, Arthur O.   F   1925-
  Making mission happen.

  Includes bibliographical references.
  1. Missions—Study and teaching. I. Title.
BV2090.B28   266'.007   74-20517
ISBN 0-377-00019-1

acknowledgments _____

The following credits express our appreciation to the publishers and writers who have allowed us to use their material in this book.

(Editor's Note: Words in brackets within quoted passages indicate a word change made to avoid any sex-role stereotyping.)

PP. 14-15, 27-28, 43-44, From pp. 56-57, 92-93, 109 in THE VALIDITY OF THE CHRISTIAN MISSION by Elton Trueblood. Copyright © 1972 by D. Elton Trueblood. By permission of Harper & Row, Publishers, Inc.
P. 15, From *From Mission to Mission* by R. Pierce Beaver. Used by permission of Association Press.
P. 16, From notes from an address by Emilio Castro delivered on October 29, 1973 to the United Methodist Board of Global Ministries. Edited text used by permission of Emilio Castro.
PP. 16-17, From #One Meditation by Edward C. May. Presented at the Zion Conference, October 28-30, 1973. Used by permission of the author.

PP. 17-18, 45-46, From *Unchanging Mission* by Douglas Webster. Used by permission of Hodder and Stoughton Limited.

PP. 21-22, From *The Message and Its Messengers* by D. T. Niles. Used by permission of Abingdon Press.

PP. 22-23, 55-56, From FOR ALL THE WORLD by John V. Taylor. Published in the United States by The Westminster Press, 1967. Copyright © 1966 by The Evangelical Fellowship in the Anglican Communion. Used by permission. British rights by permission of Hodder and Stoughton Limited.

PP. 24-26, From *Salvation Today* by Arne Sovik. Copyright 1973. Used by permission of Augsburg Publishing House.

PP. 30-32, From the statement "Declaration of World Christian Mission Witness" by the World Division of United Methodist Board of Global Ministries. Used by permission.

PP. 32-33, From the press release "New Era of Interdependence" written November 13, 1973 by the News Bureau of the Lutheran Church in America.

PP. 33-34, From *Call to Mission* by Stephen Neill. Copyright 1970. Used by permission of Fortress Press.

P. 35, From *The Go-Between God* by John V. Taylor. Copyright 1972. Used by permission of Fortress Press and SCM Press, Ltd.

PP. 37-38, From THE CHRISTIAN ENCOUNTERS THE NEW FACE OF MISSIONS by Edgar R. Trexler, copyright 1973 by Concordia Publishing House. Used by permission.

PP. 40-41, From *Yes to Mission* by Douglas Webster. Copyright 1966. Used by permission of SCM Press, Ltd.

PP. 48-49, From Inga-Brita Casteren's article "Education for Mission" in *International Review of Mission,* V. LXII, No. 245, January 1973, pp. 94-95.

PP. 53-55, Quoted from THE CENTER LETTER, Vol 3, No. 4, April, 1973, a publication of the Center for Parish Development, 329 E. School Avenue, Naperville, Illinois 60540. Used by permission.

P. 58, From the Today's English Version of the New Testament. Copyright © American Bible Society, 1966, 1971.

PP. 58-59, From *The Small Catechism* by Martin Luther. Copyright 1960. Used by permission of Fortress Press.

PP. 65-67, From *THE INTERPRETER,* published by the United Methodist Church, United Methodist Communications, 1200 Davis St., Evanston, Ill. 60201.

contents _____

in appreciation _____

Existential insight for the Christian comes slowly over the years. I am grateful for teachers, fellow pastors and colleagues and, above all, fellow Christians who can enlighten me with how God acts among people.

Special note belongs to that company of saints that nurtured me when a boy and young man at Augsburg Evangelical Lutheran Church, Toledo, Ohio. Two other congregations provided the fellowship, workshop, problems and joys for joint service: Bethesda-on-the-Bay Church in Bay Village, Ohio and Good Shepherd Church in Kenwood, Ohio.

Fellow staff members of the Division for World Mission and Ecumenism of the Lutheran Church in America have given during the last ten years, beyond their awareness, insight and encouragement about the mission of Christ's church. The "first century" Christians of churches in the Third World have taught and shown me the faith-reality of the church.

And lastly, to my wife, Danita, who encourages, analyzes and assists much beyond my fondest hopes, and two daughters, Nancy and Joanne, who enliven my days to joy-overflowing, a special word of appreciation.

introduction _____

This book aims to assist the local church in carrying on an effective mission education program. It is a practical book, giving ways and means for doing the job.

Mission, however, is a big subject. And there are many and conflicting ideas about what mission is and how mission "happens." Before undertaking mission education, the reader is asked to explore the what and why of "mission" —the "education" will follow in due course.

In exploring what mission is in our day, no one definition will be offered in these pages. Mission is in too much ferment for any one statement to be final and acceptable to all. Rather, a number of "working definitions" will be set forth, with opportunity for you and your group to evaluate them and perhaps prepare your own.

The first section of this book exposes the reader to some exciting and stimulating ideas about the mission of the church. The second section examines the local church and the role of mission education in its life. The material in the first and second sections consists of selected quotations. They represent current mission ideas presented in an easily readable manner.

The third section discusses organization, activities and resources for mission education in the local church and community. This collection is the product of reading, listening, sharing, doing—with many persons contributing.

Everyone has a bias, a focus, a viewpoint—on everything. Your author is not without one either.

The author's primary attention is not cell groups, or social action, or pastoral counseling, or transactional analysis, or some other fad. These and other matters are important and useful, but are secondary, by-products, non-essential.

My bias is the Gospel. I believe the message; I accept the Lord. Other emphases are motivated by this central focus.

The selection of quotations for this book, as well as the direction of my own writing reflects my viewpoint. I believe "mission" is not an option or a side-show, but the heart of expressing and living out the Gospel. This book tries to encourage and help the local church fulfill its real purpose.

Words are the vehicles for conveying human thought. As words change meaning or fail to express our ideas, we adjust our vocabulary, or use footnotes to explain. Mission literature carries some unfortunate baggage—words, effective at another place and day, but rude, incorrect or even offensive today. "Younger" and "older" church—what concept did that once convey? "Sending" and "receiving" —who is which, then and now? "Native" or "national"; "missionary" or "missioner"; "foreign" to whom? Where is the "Third World"? Aren't we trying to gain the vision of "one world"? And if we use "Third World," what and where are the first and second worlds? The vocabulary of this book, and of the quotations widely used, will not serve every one of us: some may well be offended. Rather than complain, or close the book, stick with it and try to discover the meaning, or select the more appropriate term for you today.

Neither the "mission ideas" nor the "mission action" suggested in this book are exhaustively expressed. Where you wish, pursue the idea, follow up by reading more of the author, or the full text which supplied the quote. Where the action seems to address your situation, discuss it with others and shape it as you see it for the specific local church. Step-by-step, hand-in-hand directions are not provided. The thought is hinted at and you "run with the ball."

This book is one to live with rather than to curl up with. All the ideas and action recommendations cannot be started or finished in one year, or even two. Make a selection, basing your plans on where your members are now and where you hope to move them.

The book title suggests action and rightly so. We want our churches alive with the excitement of God's action in the world. The theological accent, however, is not on our *doing* mission, but on our *being* mission.

Reflect on the distinction of *being* and *doing:* which comes first? which directs the other? When reflection sinks the idea into our minds, we get a new understanding of mission and our role in it. Without this serving role, without God being first, without God's action upon us, the mission is not *the* mission.

Making Mission Happen seeks to outline ideas and processes for the local church to be a part of the world church. The actor on the scene is God! Our role: to be so committed to God that we can be a willing instrument for accomplishing the mission.

John V. Taylor says, "The marching orders and the gift of the Spirit come in the same package" (*The Go-Between God,* Philadelphia: Fortress Press, 1973, p. 4). Be patient before "making mission happen." The orders and the gift should be together, and when they are, watch out for the happening!

SECTION 1

mission
panorama

1
mission imperative

The urgency of the church's mission is caught by the following writers. The distinction between "evangelism" and "development," where these are seen as mutually exclusive emphases, is a false one. The gospel demands evangelism and development, proclamation and service, care for the individual and concern for society.

WHY SHOULD WE?

"Where would any of us Christians be today

"—if the disciples had decided to stay in Jerusalem and clean up their backyard first?

"—if St. Paul had refused to accept the challenge to move from Asia Minor to Europe?

"—if St. Augustine had elected to deal with local problems first?

"—if Boniface had stayed in his English monastery instead of going forth to evangelize the barbarous people of Germany? . . .

"—if Count Nikolaus von Zinzendorf and his followers had been content to remain in Germany instead of founding their Moravian communities in the new world?

"—if David Livingstone had not been lured by the mystery of half-hidden Africa?

"Some of the names in this litany of missionary adventurers may mean nothing to many readers. Yet our own heritage as Christians, our civilization and the course of the

13

world's history has been radically influenced by their calling to serve Christ somewhere other than home."—**A. Theodore Eastman**[1]

CHIEF MOTIVE FOR MISSION

"The chief motive for the Christian Mission is best expressed in a paradox, which is the central paradox of the Gospel. We soon notice, as we study Christ's own words about the Church, that he employed a number of metaphors, of which the one about the fire is the most striking. He spoke of 'salt,' of 'light' and of 'leaven.' At first glance these seem to be very different from one another, but, as we examine them, we soon realize that they have one feature in common: *all are figures representing penetration.* The salt exists to penetrate the meat, the light exists to penetrate the darkness, and the leaven exists to penetrate the dough in order that it may rise. Each is lost, yet is, at the same time, created of something of supreme value. The most surprising fact is that each of these is frustrated in its true function whenever it is *saved,* because the essence of each is that it is radically expendable. The way to destroy the usefulness of a lamp is to try to protect it by putting it under a meal-tub (Matt. 5:15, *The New English Bible*). What we do not use we really lose!

"The central paradox about saving and losing provides the Christian Mission with its *raison d'être.* The paradox appears in all of the Synoptic Gospels, the basic statement being, 'For whoever would save his life will lose it; and whoever loses his life for my sake and the gospel's will save it' (Mark 8:35). Herein lies the essence of the theology which has made the phenomenon of Mission possible. Christianity, as has often been said, is, by its very nature, diffusive, but the doctrine of diffusion does not stand alone; it follows logically from the doctrine of expendability.

---

[1] "Notes" indicating sources of all quotes to follow begin on page 95. Biographic material on all contributors listed in "Voices in Mission" on page 93.

MISSION IMPERATIVE

"When the doctrine of expendability is fully accepted, it becomes at once obvious that, in contrast to many organizations, the Church is not instituted for the benefit of its members. Christ enlists ordinary men and women into his enduring fellowship, not primarily in order to save them, but because he has work for them to do. It is a genuine revelation that his primary call to commitment, 'Come to me,' is associated at once with a call to labor, 'Take my yoke upon you.' The Church is essential to the Christian, not because it brings personal advancement or even inspiration, but because, with all its failures, it is an indispensable instrument for the redemption of the world.

"Here is a sufficient answer to anyone who asks the reason for the missionary enterprise. Mission is not extracurricular, but represents the essential meaning of the Church as a unique fellowship."—**Elton Trueblood** [2]

NEW "CHRISTENDOM"

"The starting place for mission is the recognition that a geographical "Christendom" in the West has been replaced by a 'diffused Christendom' composed of churches and disciples all around the world. The first task [of] American church[es] is to acquaint [itself] with the young churches and get a sense of the reality of this new world-wide base of mission. Each of our local congregations is a part of it.

"There is another fact, too, which must sink home into the American Christian consciousness if our people are zealously to participate in mission. That is the truth that Christianity is not a dying religion. They must understand the magnitude of the almost miraculous growth of the churches overseas in just half a century. . . .

"God never instructed us that we were to convert every [person] on earth to the Christian faith, but he did commission us through Christ and the Holy Spirit to make disciples of all nations, and to communicate the message of reconciliation through the ministry of reconciliation."—**R. Pierce Beaver**[3]

15

IMAGING GLOBAL PERSPECTIVES

"Global means the realization of a world interaction: what you do in your local situation, the faithfulness to your local mission, is your best global service.

"Global is a dimension that respects, enriches, but never suppresses or suffocates the local.

"Global is the willingness to listen to all voices in the . . . world. . . . That means to be global, the discussing processes should be enlarged through encounters, visits, guests, letters, etc.

"Global means the pooling of resources, . . . power for rendering a better missionary service to the six continents. It is also opportunity to receive help from churches and people all over the world.

"Global means to realize the global dimensions of your nation's attitudes. A global mission means for you to act responsibily in relation to your nation's foreign policy, to investments' policy, to behavior of big corporations, to the shaping of a sound public opinion. Because you are global, you assume responsibility for the global attitudes of your nation."—**Emilio Castro**[4]

WHERE THE FIELD?

"Read the parable of the Good Samaritan to any Christian in North America, and almost immediately that person identifies with the Good Samaritan. On rare occasions of repentance, the person might identify with the priest or levite, but seldom, if ever, conceives himself [or herself] as the person in the ditch—the one who needs help!

"Speak the Savior's word, 'The fields are ripe for harvest; pray the Lord of the harvest to send laborers into the harvest,' and Christians in North America identify with the laborers who are to do the harvesting—but not with the ripened grain which needs attention.

"Lead a study on the book of Acts and a Christian in North America gets a vicarious thrill out of identifying with the Apostle Paul, seeing him- or herself as an adventurer among people of other lands and cultures. But seldom have

Christians imagined themselves uttering the Macedonian cry, 'Come and help us!'

"We are to see ourselves not in our customary self-appointed roles of Good Samaritan, of laborers in the harvest field, or those answering the call for help—but as victims, as ripened grain, as Macedonians crying for help."—**Edward C. May**[5]

AN UNFINISHED AND INESCAPABLE TASK

"The unfinished tasks remaining for the defense of human rights are huge, terribly hard, and at the same time, cannot be postponed any longer. Millions of valuable lives must be freed from hunger and oblivion, millions of homes saved from destruction, and thousands of lives must be rescued from torture and death. This is why Christians must move from an attitude of innocence or passivity to one of critical consciousness, involvement.

"Christians are called to utilize all the resources available to correct the situations of oppression, persecution or injustice that we discover. Christians are called to denounce all of these flagrant violations of the rights of [people] through the media, through appeals to all concerned international Church and secular organizations. Christians are called to use imagination and energy to organize plans of action to defend those affected by injustice."—**Federico Pagura**[6]

DOWNWARD REACH

"We cannot demythologize the love of God or the cross of Christ, the gift of forgiveness or the gift of the Spirit. The heart of the Gospel is in eternal and unchanging categories. The essential Gospel is about love, truth, faith, hope, joy, peace, anxiety, sin, death, judgment, wisdom, power, reconciliation. There is an enormous area which cannot and will not be demythologized or diminished. Either we have the Gospel whole and given or we have no Gospel at all.

"Our supreme need is not a new strategy of mission but

17

a new inspiration for mission, which can come only from a new and much deeper grasp of the Gospel."—**Douglas Webster**[7]

STUDY QUESTIONS

1. "Mission Imperative" illustrates the need for mission, but what does "mission" mean? Begin to formulate your own definition. Suppose that you are a member of a task group commissioned to determine the mission policy of your denomination for the next five years. Below is a list of assumptions about mission. Read through the list. Draw a line through those statements with which you cannot agree. Rank order the remaining statements by writing a number *one* beside the assumption you feel is most important, a number *two* beside the second most important assumption, etc. until you reach number *six*. Compare your list with those of other persons.

Mission means
  Preaching the Gospel to the heathen
  Going to a foreign country
  Liberating the oppressed
  Converting people to our way of life
  Helping the unfortunate
  Brotherhood among all races and classes
  Raising money to send missionaries
  Witnessing to Jesus wherever we are
  Supporting people who help themselves
  Being sensitive to other people's way of life
  A spiritual Gospel: nothing to do with politics or economics
  Listening to the questions people ask
  Recognizing our interdependence with others
  Working for community: includes economics and politics
  Loving our neighbor

(Adapted from *Mission Impossible—Unless* . . . by Cyril Powles and Rob Nelson, © 1973 by Friendship Press.)

2. State in your own words Trueblood's definition of the motive for mission. What is your personal biblical reference for the motive for mission? Check your response with Trueblood's definition. Then check both statements with one other person. Now write a new statement on which you and the other person can agree.

3. Do you agree with Emilio Castro's statements on "imaging global perspectives?" Where do you agree or disagree and why? Think of a project your church assumes locally. Have you made a connection between local and global mission in regard to this one project? How did you do it? What did you find out? What about individual self-image, imagining one's self as in mission: What helps or hinders this self-imaging?

4. Castro mentions mission on six continents. Identify the six continents.

5. Castro says one aspect of global mission means the opportunity to receive help from churches and people all over the world. Do you agree? Look in your church papers, and ask your minister if any church or "project" in our country has received help from another country? Where? What form did it take—a missionary from the Third World serving in your area? A pastor or associate pastor in a nearby church from another country? A youth serving as an exchange student who feels a commitment to global education in the school and community? Money from overseas given to a special emergency in our country?

6. In what ways do you think getting involved in local mission would help people support global mission?

7. What about Castro's last sentence—assuming responsibility for global attitudes of our country? Look in newspapers and news magazines for a quote from a national figure that does or does not give evidence of a global concern. Write a letter to that person reacting to the point of view expressed. Take one national issue relating to action that Castro mentions in the last paragraph and consider what your personal opinion is, what your own church has said about it, and what stand a national board of your

church has taken in relation to that issue. Follow through on that one issue for a period of weeks or months and point out to a concerned group of persons in your church what steps can be taken to express global concern on this one issue.

8. Name three human rights as stated in the Declaration of Human Rights. How is your church or our country living up to those rights? Specifically where has it failed? What can you do individually? The entire congregation? (Order a copy of the Declaration of Human Rights.

2
mission theology

Theological discussion is an inherent part of mission. The following authors present ideas to make us think, but not necessarily to agree. Our minds are to be stretched in the exploration.

FAITH AND ACTION

"The danger which some Christians face, as they discover the need for a deep devotional life, is to assume that this alone is all that God asks. Then we must remember several of Christ's most pointed words, 'Inasmuch as you did it to the least of these. . . ,' 'Ye shall be my witnesses. . .' 'Not the one who says Lord, Lord, but the one who does the will of my father.' God sent Jesus into the midst of a world in turmoil—a time with strange parallels to our own. Jesus prayed and worshipped and lived in close communion with his father. But most of the time he was out on the dusty roads of Palestine, healing the sick, comforting the broken hearted, feeding the hungry, rebuking the powerful who oppressed the poor. He was demonstrating, as well as saying, that God cares very much about people and the world and every aspect of life. As his disciples, we are called to the same kind of action today. We need to be out in our neighborhoods, and cities, and nation, and world, giving our time, energy and talents to helping those in need and changing society so that justice and freedom and opportunity are available to all of God's children."—**Cynthia Wedel** [8]

THE CHURCH AS ANSWER

"The answer to the problems of the world is the answer that Jesus Christ provided, which is the Church. Jesus has set in the world a community bound to him, sharing his life and his mission, and endued with the power of the Holy Spirit. This community is the answer that Jesus has provided for the evils of this world. It is we who in our common life should demonstrate the possibilities of reconciliation and peace between people, who in our common mission should demonstrate the direction along which history is set, who in our common hope should be able to rescue [people] from despair and frustration. This is the answer which Jesus provided and which we betray when we are disloyal to him."—**D. T. Niles**[9]

SIGNS OF THE UNIVERSAL CHURCH

"Missionaries are remembrancers of the unfinished task both to those churches to which they go and to those from which they come. In this respect their furlough is as much a part of their obedience as is their service overseas. But they are remembrancers also of the 'Christian International,' of the Church which transcends culture and race. In this respect their foreignness is the particular asset which they bring. They are signs of the new [person] in which the distinctions between Greek and Jew, circumcision and uncircumcision, Barbarian and Scythian, slave and free man, no longer signify, but Christ is all in all. As such they are part of the evidence to the world vindicating the Gospel which they preach.

"If the foreign missionary is needed to contribute the sign of his [or her] foreignness to a church's participation in the Mission, then it follows that every church needs foreign missionaries to complete its presentation of the Gospel. D.T. Niles has said that the church in Asia has enjoyed the strength of receiving missionaries, but until recently, has suffered the weakness of not having sent them; while the church in the West has enjoyed the strength of having sent missionaries, but suffers the grave weakness of never having received them. Both need to make good their deficiency. Already the Methodist Church in Ceylon [now Sri Lanka] has sent its missionaries to East Africa, Korean Christians are laboring in Thailand, Japanese evangelists are preaching in Southeast Asia, Filipino teachers are going to Indonesia, and the Church of South India has missionaries in more than six countries. In Britain we have welcomed evangelists from East Africa who have brought revival to some of our churches; many parishes have been inspired by the ministry of Africans or Asians who have come on short visits as assistant clergy. But all these things are only a beginning, and we look forward with expectancy to that richer and more permanent interchange of missionary partnership which alone can be adequate to bring the Gospel to our strangely international world."—**John V. Taylor**[10]

GEOGRAPHICAL MYTH

"It is the whole world, and not any specified geographical segments of it, that is the mission field of the church. There is only one world and only one church for it. If the missionary frontier is conceived in purely geographical terms, conceivably the mission of the church might eventually be finished.

"The geographical frontier can have meaning and evocative power for missionary obedience if it is understood as a symbol—a symbol of the *total* mission of the one church to the one world. The present task is to draw out the implications of the symbol in such a way that the whole church, wherever it is locally manifested, becomes aware that *it* is in the mission field—the world—and that *it* has the missionary task of carrying the gospel to any and all frontiers. One aspect of the oneness of the church is that every part of the church is at one with the other parts in missionary engagement in the world. In this sense, churches cannot have missions. The church as a whole cannot *have* missions—the implication being that it might *not* have. The church *is* mission. Wherever the church meets the world, *there* is the missionary frontier. And when it crosses frontiers, horizontal or vertical, it does so, not as a "mission," but as the church. Indeed, it is thus that the church proves that it *is* the church."—**Keith R. Bridston**[11]

SALVATION: PERSONAL OR SOCIAL

The following quotation relates to the World Council of Churches conference on "Salvation Today" held in Bangkok, January 1973. Highly important voices were heard there; they will influence mission thought greatly for the next decade.

"Wherever the subject of God's salvation is discussed, however the idea is approached, one problem arises: if salvation is not simply an inner spiritual event, but also has its social life-related aspect, how are these two related? The question can be posed in many ways. How is salvation as change *in* [a person] related to salvation as change *around* [a person]? How is salavation as regeneration, [a person's] 'being-born-againness' and therefore his [or her] capacity to transcend environment, related to salvation as transforming or at least maintaining order in the environment? Or, practically, how are evangelism and development, proclamation and social justice related?

"Whatever the political and religious structures have been, an acceptable theological formulation has always been difficult to work out. The tendency to over-emphasize God's saving activity in Christ as a purely spiritual and inner and other-worldly matter has led to the famous description of religion as the 'opiate of the people,' a comfort to be sure, but hardly an effective force in the struggle for a more just society. The other tendency, to emphasize the social-ethical-political aspect of Christianity to the exclusion of the spiritual, inner element, can make of the church little more than a political party and can lead to the absolutizing, or idolizing of political systems by claiming for them divine authority and support.

"The one emphasis spiritualizes and personalizes the

24

message of the Scriptures. It finds in the liberation of the Hebrews from Egypt an allegory of the spiritual life, forgetting that here were real people whom God in history really delivered from slavery to another nation. The other emphasis sees the saving effects of the gospel first of all in social ethics, the improvement of society, the enrichment of life, and finds in the Old Testament prophet rather than the New Testament evangelist the prototype of the Christian preacher.

"How did the early Christians solve this problem of the relationship of the personal and the social aspects of salvation? They seem to have withdrawn briefly from society to live in their own community until the Lord came. But this experiment in a counter-cultural social salvation did not last long. Countless other attempts at righteous communities have been made; but none have solved the problem. Bangkok cannot be said to have resolved this intractable problem either. It is possible that one reason was the lack of prominence given to the word *love* in our debates. But Bangkok struggled with three other words that seemed to speak of salvation to modern [humanity].

"These three concepts of salvation, among many others, have been emphasized in the current discussion. Each of them can be used to describe both the inner, spiritual salvation and the outer, temporal salvation. They are the concepts of *liberation, humanness* and *identity*. . . .

"*Liberation* is the poor [person's] definition of salvation. It is the cry of the powerless, the prayer of the oppressed. What is striking about the spiritual, however, is that its cry for liberation rises from the throats of a liberated people: salvation is here paradoxically demanded by the saved. . . .

"What does it mean to be *human*? The common response to that question is that it is to be weak: 'I'm only human.' Or on the other hand omnipotent: 'The people,' says Mao Tse-tung, 'are God.' Or to have rights: 'I'm a human being!' But biblically to be human is to be created in the image of God—dependent, contingent to be sure, but endowed with a transcendent character derived from God and binding the human person to the Creator. The religious and the atheist alike recognize that [people] fail to live up to the image [they have of themselves]. That, so to speak, the *fully human* is never attained. . . .

"The air is full these days of psychological terms. One of the most frequently heard and most powerfully emotive is the term *identity*. In this day of mobility, of uncertainty and agnosticism, of loneliness and alienation and all the melancholy consequences of an individualism gone mad, it is the name attached to that which is most basic. To be saved is to find the answer to that elemental question: Who am I? . . . .

"What is salvation? Many things, but also at least these three: liberation, humanness, identity.

"It is with these understandings of salvation (and the others) then that the church must concern itself; for salvation is the business of the church, its mission in the world."
—Arne Sovik[12]

THE ISSUE IS JUSTICE

" 'The new name for peace is development,' says the Pope. 'Development is what is not happening fast enough in today's world,' says the World Council of Churches. More than half the people of the world lack nourishing food, are crippled physically and mentally by malnutrition early in life and are made incapable of effective work because of low energy and susceptibility to disease. What is to be done in this age of science, with its apparent promise of unlimited possibilities? Can the world share its wealth on some equitable basis? What would be involved?

"Gradually the world has come to realize that justice is no longer a national family affair but a problem of world politics. The rich and powerful peoples have been made sharply aware of the poor and powerless. We are beginning to realize at last that the solution lies not in endless shipments of food to the hungry or clothes to the ragged, worthy though such actions are, but in a political and social and economic revolution on a worldwide scale. Ultimately this revolution is going to mean a redistribution of the world's resources—and *potential* resources. It will be part of a new and just world order based on the solidarity of all [people] and all nations.

"The church of Jesus Christ is set in this world. Its own search for unity and renewal will be fruitless so long as the world is rent asunder. It cannot remain splendidly aloof on the top of a pillar in a far-off desert, meditating on 'spiritual things.' And it cannot sit on the riverbank watching the flood roar by. It has to plunge in where humanity is, to share its turmoil and suffering. Sympathy is not enough. The renewal of the church means *engagement* in the struggles of the world."—**Pieter M. Bouman**[13]

WHAT DO YOU MEAN, MISSIONS?

"It is dismaying that twentieth century Christians should have problems with the words: *mission, missions, missionary*. Our shyness about these words may be wrapped up in our ignorance and uneasiness about the history of missions and in our uncertainty about their future. Our discomfort is an indication that we are caught in an age of transition where old landmarks have lost their meaning and new ones are yet to be discovered.

"Christians understand their overall mission (singular) to be cooperation with God in his activity of wooing the world to put its final trust in him alone, as he is revealed in Jesus Christ. Missions (plural) describe specific assignments within the divine-human compact of cooperation. Missionaries are those Christians who in one way or another contract to cooperate with God."—**A. Theodore Eastman**[14]

DEFENSE OF MISSION

"Wherein does the validity of the Christian Mission rest? If it is dependent upon social service, it may be convincing for awhile, but it is not likely to be permanently so.

"The ultimate and permanent case for the Christian Mission rests directly upon the conception that the Christian faith is true. This is the one point which the critics of the enterprise do not touch, except by such an undermining of truth as undermines even their own criticism. In the long run, the best reason for dedication to the spread of the faith of Christ is the conviction that the faith conforms to reality as does no other alternative of which we are aware. Such a position is bound, in our age of supposed tolerance and religious pluralism, to be widely unpopular, but that is not a sufficient reason for rejecting it. If Christianity is not true, there is certainly no adequate reason to reach people with its message, whether they live in China or in California. All of the service tasks can finally be handled in other ways, but the central message of Christ can be handled in only one way, i.e., by committed ambassadors. If the message is not true, the Mission will die and really ought to die; it cannot be maintained permanently by auxiliary enterprises."—**Elton Trueblood** [15]

STUDY QUESTIONS

1. Interview one young person and one adult in your church, asking them to name and describe one specific way your church is "out in the *neighborhood* . . . giving time, energy and talents to helping others and changing society." Then ask for one specific way your church is out in the *nation* and the *world* giving time, energy and talents to helping others and to changing society. If you are involved in a group study put the responses on newsprint, look for the gaps, revise and decide to take one firm step toward advancing justice and freedom to your community.
2. Look in your church magazines or write your mission board to find out what exchange of missionaries exists in your denomination and where they are serving. Make this information available to the congregation.
3. Take a poll in your church asking the question, "Would you be willing to have a minister or associate minister from another country serve in this church? Why or why not?"
4. Give one sentence clarifying what is meant by the statement "The new name for peace is development." Test with

someone and write a new sentence together.

5. Can you describe the tension between "proclamation" and "development" (witness and service) as seen in the mission enterprise?

6. Distinguish between "mission" and "missions."

7. What would be one way you would educate children, youth and adults in your church about the implications for Christians in the words, justice—liberation—development? Relate your answer to your concept of education for mission.

8. Write 50 words stating what you believe this section is saying about the mission of the Christian.

9. How are the ideas of liberation and mission linked?

10. Add one illustration of your own to Keith Bridston's list in the section, "The Vocational Myth."

3
mission strategy

How does the church go about its mission task? What are the issues to be faced? The following quotations address such matters.

MISSION AS WORLD-WIDE FAITH

"Now that Christianity has been planted and has taken root in almost every soil under the sun, the sorting out and sloughing off process is accelerating rapidly. Gothic architecture, Western forms of worship and alien patterns of action, for example, are being replaced. Other Christians are helping us Westerners see what is at the heart of our faith and what is not. Other cultures are making their own contributions to the universal acceptance and understanding of the gospel, so that we are learning much about our faith from those whom our grandfathers evangelized. This is the thrill of living in the first phase of the ecumenical age.

"[People are] searching for universal truth, not partial truth. [We] need final answers to the enigmas of life, not solutions that apply to one segment of humanity only. [We are] seeking to know and serve the one, all-powerful God, not a local deity whose influence ends at the shore of this ocean or that continent. If the Christian gospel isn't true for all people in all places at all times, then it isn't very good news for anyone who lives in a world we know to be one."—**A. Theodore Eastman**[16]

WORLD CHRISTIAN MISSION IS . . .

"World Christian mission is the Christian's response to the mandate of the Gospel to be worthy witnesses to the

30

Good News that God is alive in the world and in society. Christian mission affirms by declaration and in action God's perpetual care for all people and for the world.

"1. *World Christian Mission Witnesses to the Universal Lordship of Jesus Christ.* The imperative is to communicate the Good News of Jesus Christ as Lord and Savior of all people and societies. Persons and communities must have the opportunity to hear about Jesus Christ, to study the meaning of the Christ event for themselves and their world, and to respond to him in the commitment of faith and action.

"The Christian community will undertake the task of witness to Jesus Christ by word and deed, by preaching, individual conversations, worship, service, struggle in Christ's name for justice and freedom for all, dialogue with persons of other faiths, and participation in secular movements that seek fuller life for all.

"The belief that Jesus is Lord is central today to all we do in mission.

"2. *World Christian Mission is Interchurch Assistance and Mutual Support.* Christian communities around the world, in the free exercise of their self-determination, need assistance. Resources from areas of the world where the Christian community shares in economic affluence and its many trained persons must be made available when these are urgently requested by some other Christian community of the world. Such resources are shared not to direct the life of another church, but to support that church in its life, growth and witness. The growing movement of overseas churches towards autonomy, already a fact in many areas, is a healthy development that puts direction of the church's life in the hands of those closest to the place of mission, but autonomy does not relieve us of support of those who continue to need and request assistance we can provide.

"The Christian communities to which we relate are both denominational and interdenominational, and include the people of God at work in very secular and non-ecclesiastical programs.

"3. *World Christian Mission is the Liberation of People for the Transformation of their Societies and for the Achievement of their Highest Potential.* The task of mission focuses continually on the preparation of persons to be what by God's grace they may come to be. Persons must be freed from weights of hunger, oppression, ignorance and fear in order to participate individually and collectively in the call God directs to each person. Education is central to mission, it being understood that education is meant in broad context, including formal and informal schooling, educational programs of the local church and more.

"Liberation is both personal and societal. One contributes to the other. The Christian community seeks to assist individuals and societies to find a multitude of expressions of genuine responsible freedom under Christ which will assist all towards a fuller human life of meaning and service.

"4. *World Christian Mission is Participation in National and World Development.* Loving service is inherent in Christian mission and witness. Such love seeks to perform the compassionate act where needed, and also to get at roots of national and world problems which bear on human life. Thus Christian mission is deeply concerned with the difficult issues of social justice, self-reliance and economic development. In national and international forums people seek corporate relationships which will contribute to the common good and to the liberation of all humankind. Christian mission seeks out the points where it can most helpfully identify with national and international searches for development in its widest meaning.

"Participation in development is an expression of Christian faith in the midst of the affairs of peoples and communities. It goes far beyond mere social action to seek the abundance of life for which Jesus Christ lived and died."
—United Methodist Church[17]

NEW ERA OF "INTERDEPENDENCE"

"An 'independence/interdependence' course in its world mission operation has been set in principle by the Management Committee of the Division for World Mission and Ecumenism of the Lutheran Church in America.

"The Division is now entering a 'new era,' the Rev. Dr. David Vikner, executive director of the Division, said in a background paper.

" 'Though every generation since the Renaissance/Reformation believed that it faced a turning point in history, it is increasingly evident with the unprecedented explosions of our time—in knowledge, communications, production, as well as pollution, population and the means of mass destruction—that we are at one of those historic corners.'

"He describes this new era in world mission, also referred to as 'Stage Three,' as one in which 'independent, autonomous, self-reliant partners interdependently share their resources.'

" 'Stage Three' follows Stage One or 'mission era' in which missionaries were sent out on a ministry of teaching, preaching and healing and the Christian church was established 'in nearly every country on earth,' and Stage Two in which the younger churches born and developed in Stage One 'became autonomous, elected their own national leaders and staffed most of their churches and institutions with indigenous personnel.'

"In setting its new course the Division also asked that steps be taken in North America to increase 'global consciousness and the thrust of six continent mission' including such things as Christians from other parts of the world 'serving as missionaries to the United States as American missionaries serve in their countries' and younger churches making financial grants 'towards mission projects in the United States.' "—**David L. Vikner**[18]

The following four quotations discuss various aspects of the missionary vocation, illustrating the dynamic changes underway in this facet of the mission enterprise.

MISSIONARY OF THE FUTURE

"The radical nature of the change is briefly expressed in the new slogan, 'mission in six continents,' which is highly popular today. This slogan may be criticized as blurring outlines and overlooking differences of which account still has to be taken. Mission in the run-down areas of Philadelphia and Chicago may be even more difficult than in Cairo or Bangkok; but the problem of approaching with the Gospel those who have been conditioned all their lives by a non-Christian culture and religion is not the same as that of making the Gospel real to those who live on the margins of a civilization that bears a profound Christian impress. It is misleading when such differences are overlooked. But what the slogan does effectively make clear is that mission is not something that allegedly Christian countries can impose on an unhappy heathen world. Mission is something that all churches are engaged in all the time. Every church, for the sake of its own health, must be both a sending and a receiving church. Wherever a church exists, older or younger, stronger or weaker, richer or poorer, there is the potential center of mission.

"It should occasion no surprise that leaders in some younger churches, flushed with their new sense of spiritual freedom, resentful of the patronizing and domineering attitude of some missionaries in the past, and unwilling to risk any encroachments on their hardwon independence, say frankly that now the current should flow in the other direction. The younger churches, with their greater vigor and the freshness of their faith, are now called to help the older churches to recover the vision that they have so largely lost and to become again living members in the body of Christ. Voices such as those of Toyohiko Kagawa, D. T. Niles, and a host of others have aroused the West by their prophetic quality. It is possible gratefully to recognize this new store of spiritual riches which God has given to the churches in our time, and yet to think that the current should still flow in both directions, that the older churches in the West still have a responsibility in relation both to the younger churches and to the non-Christian world which still stands outside the sphere of Christian influence."
—**Stephen Neill**[19]

SPIRIT LED

"We can see now the enormous breadth and range of
the mission of the Creator Spirit. It embraces the plant
geneticist breeding a new strain of wheat, the World Health
Organization team combating bilharzia, the reconstruction
company throwing a bridge across a river barrier, the political pressure group campaigning for the downfall of a cor-
rupt city council, the amateur dramatics group in the new
cultural center, the team on the new oil-rig, the parents'
committee fighting for desegregated schools in the inner
city. The missionaries of the Holy Spirit include the proba-
tion officer and the literacy worker, the research chemist
and the worn-out school teacher in a remote village, the
psychiatrist and the designer, the famine-relief worker and
the computer operator, the pastor and the astronaut. Our
theology of mission will be all wrong unless we start with a
song of praise about this surging diversity of creative and
redemptive initiative."—**John V. Taylor**[20]

VOCATIONAL MYTH

"Can the mission of the church be symbolically revita-
lized? Is it possible for the church to resymbolize its apostolic character through other means than the foreign missionary movement itself if that movement disappears?

"Symbols are not thought out. They are lived out. This is
the ever-new missionary challenge facing the church.

" • A young Dutchman and his wife sit in a small cottage
on an Indonesian island. They are the last remnants of a
political empire. They are the last representatives of the
Western missionary enterprise. They do nothing. They organize nothing. They run nothing. They are simply there.
And the fact of their presence may be a more vivid symbol
of the true meaning of Christian love, of the ultimate significance of the Christian mission, to Christians and non-
Christians alike, than all the 'Christian civilization' and
'Christian evangelization' with which nationals have been
forcibly confronted for the previous three centuries.

" • An English bishop in India leaves the mission field to which he had offered his life and devotion, to return to the West as an ecclesiastical bureaucrat and ordinary strap-hanging commuter so that his Indian colleagues can assume their responsibilities as leaders of their church. His leaving more than his coming symbolizes to many the meaning of Christian apostolate.

" • The bishop of an Indonesian church, prematurely grayed by years of revolution and social and economic turmoil, turns down offers to go abroad for study or work in order that he may continue the thankless job of tending the flock, his mission.

" • Not counting the cost, a gifted professional illustrator devotes his artistic talents and imaginative craftsmanship to the service of an ecumenical agency. His drawings and designs and photographs literally symbolize the worldwide *oikumene*.

" • A Congregational minister with the warmth of human friendship and rare pastoral intuition forms a unique personal bridge between the church and the alienated worlds of culture and the arts in the intellectual milieu of New York City. The foolishness of preaching is accented, for his work is done without words—with little appreciation or financial support.

" • A West Indian pastor, former legal assistant, ecumenical administrator, evangelist in backwoods Haiti, serves an English missionary society as a board secretary and symbolizes the missionary interdependence of the new ecumenical era.

" • A Chinese priest leaves the West to return to the revolutionary ambiguities of his homeland, becoming a bishop and theological professor, a new-style missionary martyr whose natural identification with his field camouflages the intrinsic alienation from both East and West of those who proclaim the Word.

" • An Episcopal lawyer, newly out of Harvard, immerses himself in the shadowy streets of Harlem and so indentifies himself with its voiceless oppressed that his spoken and written polemics become one of their strong weapons in dispersing their darkness.

" • The dean of a theological school loses his position because his championing of the rights of a minority group student alienates the academic principalities and ecclesiastical powers.

" • An African doctor, trained in North America, puts aside his sterile surgeon's mask and spotless antiseptic gloves and enters the turbulent, 'contaminated' arena of politics to become a cabinet minister in his new nation's government—as an act of Christian vocation.

"True apostolic signs always say the exact same thing."
—Keith R. Bridston[21]

LAY PEOPLE ALIVE

"Their names are hard to pronounce. But Severo Wosoro, Shugate Dada and Abagoli Wosoro, are evangelists in Ethiopia. When the Sudan Interior Mission entered southern Ethiopia in the early 1930s, it made contact with these three members of the Kembatta tribe. But before the missionaries could develop contacts with large groups of people, the Italians invaded Ethiopia, and the missionaries were forced to flee the country.

"Since the three men were literates, they started a school and taught people to read the Bible. Before long, Abagoli became such a zealous evangelist that he was traveling the length and breadth of Kembattaland preaching and converting people. At times he was arrested and jailed by the Italians and later by the Ethiopian government. After questioning, they let him go, deciding that such a barely literate fellow was too ignorant to cause any trouble.

"Abagoli didn't cause trouble. But when the missionaries of the Sudan Interior Mission returned to Ethiopia after World War II, they discovered 50,000 converts who could be traced to the work of the three men. The Kembatta synod is now a part of the Mekane Yesus Church.

"The lesson to be learned—and it may come as a shock to some of America's ordained clergy—is the lay people in

Africa, Indonesia, Peru, New Guinea, India and a number of other countries are largely responsible for the church's rapid growth in their areas. 'I can't think of a single congregation in the last two years that was organized by an ordained pastor,' a Methodist missionary told me on the Indonesian island of Sumatra."—**Edgar R. Trexler**[22]

GLOBAL PERSPECTIVE

"*A poverty line* dangerously divides [humankind]. It lies in the northern hemisphere and follows approximately the thirtieth parallel—except that in Asia it swings north to follow the Russian boundary. It divides the United States from Latin America, Europe from Africa, Russia from the rest of Asia. Except for China, it separates the temperate from the tropical. North of that line the majority population is white, with a mixed record in racial relations; south of it the majority is black, with a vivid memory of white racial arrogance. (The largest white group in the south is Latin American, with no less vivid memories of Yankee imperialism.) North of that line lie the major strongholds of the Christian faith; south of it, the historic strongholds of the non-Christian faiths. To the north are the most rapidly growing economies; to the south, the most rapidly growing populations. To the north are history's most massive concentrations of prosperity; to the south, history's most massive concentrations of poverty. The same contrasts appear along the thirtieth parallel in the southern hemisphere. . . .

"A new kind of famine is approaching, and the decisive battle on hunger focuses on the poverty line in the northern hemisphere. Heretofore, famines have arisen from transient causes, such as drought, and have been both temporary and local. The famines of the near future will be chronic and regional, and their impact will be catastrophic.

"To some degree, this new pattern of famine is already here. One half billion persons suffer crippling hunger, and 12,000 die each day of starvation.*

---

* These figures represent research compiled in 1968.

"A billion more are undernourished. At present trends India, Iran, Indonesia, Pakistan, Turkey and perhaps China will be in several years areas of chronic famine. In Africa and Latin America, the Far East and Oceania per capita food production is below the 1939 level. Half the world's children of preschool age are so undernourished that their physical and mental growth is retarded. Yet, even the present tragedy is small compared to the catastrophe that is approaching, as population growth outraces food production.

"This condition of endemic famine is not an isolated phenomenon. The economic contrasts north and south of the world's poverty line show in many indices. Consider two of them:

" • 20 percent of [humankind] living mostly near the North Atlantic, receives nearly 80 percent of the world's income from trade and investments.

" • the average annual income in the industrialized (northern) nations is $1,900; in the agrarian (tropical belt) nations, $130.

"The ominous contrast between north and south is increasing. Population growth is greatest where the food shortage is most severe; almost twice as fast in the developing as in the affluent nations. (The 900 million people in the northern affluent nations increases at the rate of 1.2 percent a year, the 2,400 million in the developing nations at the rate of 2.2 percent a year. The current economic growth rate in the United States is about 5 percent; in the developing nations about one percent.)

"Moreover, the ability of the poorer nations to develop economies that can compete in world trade is disastrously diminished by the 'brain drain' to the northern nations. Probably 90 percent of the Asian students who come to the United States to study never return home."—**Eugene L. Smith** [23]

WHAT IS JUSTICE?

"Justice does not mean that everyone must possess the same quantity of things. That would be awful. It would be as if everyone would have the same face, the same body, the same voice. I believe in the right to have different faces and bodies. By justice I understand a better distribution of estates, at a national or international scale. There are two types of colonialism: one is internal, the other external. About this last one it is enough to say that 80 percent of the resources of the planet are in the hands of 20 percent of the countries. In order to demonstrate the internal colonialism, it's enough to speak of Brazil. There are certain zones in my country which one cannot define as underdeveloped: this would be too generous; there the people live as in the prehistoric times in caverns and they are happy if they can find anything to eat among the rubbish. What can I say to them? That they must suffer so that they may go to Paradise? Eternity starts here on Earth, not in Paradise."—**Dom Helder Camara**[24]

MISSION IS NOT

" 'Mission is not the kindness of the lucky to the unlucky,' says the Anglican document on Mutual Responsibility and Interdependence, issued by the Toronto Congress in 1963. Mission has constantly suffered from being confused with charity and relief. The motive appealed to has too often been that of compassion rather than obedience or witness. Missions are not another form of slumming—slumming at a distance by a series of substitutes who do the work for us. Human need is not to be measured in terms of income. The rich also need the Gospel of Jesus Christ and the free gift of new life in him.

"Among the educated and the well-to-do there are needs of another kind than poverty and hunger. All over Africa and Asia there are hundreds of thousands of university students, often living between two worlds, a village past and a scientific present; their situation is schizophrenic, the consequent emotional tension and strain immense. They do not generally need our money; they do need Christ. There are countless business people and civil servants, torn between the temptation to dishonesty and easy gain and a conscience about integrity. There are the masses of the disenchanted, who looked for happiness and opportunity in their newly independent countries, when the rule of the foreign imperialist was removed, but have found neither; and they live without roots and without religion and without hope—and they exist in every country. None of the millions represented by these groups can be sufficiently helped by money alone, and some have no need of money at all. Their problems will be met only on a quite different level, as were those of a lame beggar long ago. 'I have no silver or gold, but what I have I give you, in the name of Jesus Christ of Nazareth, walk' (Acts 3:6). . . .

"It is not being suggested that money does not matter. Money is needed on an enormous scale. It is a Christian duty to raise and give money to the needy millions, and organizations are doing this superbly. It is a profoundly Christian thing to do. But this is not mission. The discharge of mission requires money to support it, because it depends on living agents. But mission is not the same as knitting clothes and providing money. The sooner this myth is exploded and disposed of, the better will be the chance for church people to discover what mission really is."—**Douglas Webster**[25]

STUDY QUESTIONS

1. What is the role of the missionary today?
2. Using a globe and a length of string mark the poverty line around the world as described by Eugene L. Smith. Make a poster of facts and implications about that line. Then make available to youth and adult groups in your church a display of the globe and poster.
3. Using Dom Helder Camara's question, "What is justice?" write three sentences substituting illustrations from the USA or Canada in place of the illustrations on Brazil.
4. Do you agree with Webster's description of what "mission is not?" How would you change it? Check your response with one other person.

SECTION II

the local church and mission

1
insights

The local church everywhere is a principal manifestation of the body of Christ. Here are quotations relating the local to the universal mission.

LOCALISM

If Christians are to be liberated for creative involvement in global responsibilities, structural change is most needed in the *local parish.* Bangkok had this to say: 'The great deterrent of the mission of the local church is the ordinary Christian's lack of convictions about the relevance of Jesus Christ to the life of the world. This calls for nothing less than a conversion from parochial self-absorption to an awareness of what God is doing for the salvation of [people] in the life of the world. So any joint action in mission must be accompanied by a steady *conscientization* of local congregations.'

"The local congregation which demonstrates the healing and liberating power of the Gospel at work in its own members and in the relationships of the local community is the most effective visual aid for the Kingdom."—**James A. Scherer**[26]

STRENGTH OF A MINISTRY

"There is no way to exaggerate the potential strength of a ministry which combines evangelical theology with fearless mentality and a genuine concern for people. Those who settle for emphasis upon liturgy or activism or detached intellectuality are missing a marvelous opportunity.

The Christian leadership that can make a real difference in our time, and the time immediately ahead, will combine the Christ-centeredness of Samuel Shoemaker with the tough rationality of C. S. Lewis and the social realism of Reinhold Niebuhr. What is really foolish is to suppose that this combination is an impossible dream."—**Elton Trueblood** [27]

MISSIONAL VISION

"The New Testament concept of the church is full of joy and excitement and unbounded expectation of what God can do. Peter addresses the Christians as 'a people claimed by God for his own,' he also calls them 'a chosen race, a royal priesthood, a dedicated nation.'

"What a contrast between this magnificent concept of Christ and his church and the actual image projected by the average congregation. Instead of explosive excitement at being the people through whom God's purpose of saving all creation will be accomplished, one finds a rugged sense of duty and a mild satisfaction in small accomplishments. The image many congregations have of themselves is decidedly non-missional, and the spirit of their congregational life lacks the deep excitement of those who have discovered the pearl of great price.

"The non-missional image the local congregation has of itself is illustrated by the comparative ease with which it can raise substantial funds for local comforts such as a bigger organ, new carpets or pew cushions, and the difficulty with which it can raise even modest sums for mission outreach.

"The non-missional self-understanding of the individual Christian is apparent in the fact that not many see their day-to-day work as being a part of God's saving activity for [humanity]. Too few when choosing their work ask the basic question: How can I best use the skills and resources God has given me in his saving purposes for all [people]?"
—**E. H. Johnson**[28]

OUTWARD THRUST

"One of the new things emerging today is a recognition that every congregation must have a missionary structure. Formerly mission was regarded as a responsibility charged by the Church centrally and done through specialists. The Church expressed its outward thrust by sending missionaries overseas, and possibly by having certain home missions in the slums of great cities, on our behalf and in our stead. The local congregation was expected to do little more than contribute to the funds. And the majority of congregations were not seriously involved even that far. Now however, we are seeing that the Church's outward thrust can only be a reality if every congregation also accepts a missionary responsibility for its own neighborhood. The congregation is the primary missionary unit. It is an accurate statement to regard every congregation as missionary in its nature, for this is just what it is meant to be, whether it rises to its vocation or not. This is the calling of the congregation as a whole, and its structure is meant to be shaped with this in view.

"A corollary to this is the missionary significance of the laity. The laity are constantly thought of in negative terms as those who do not happen to be clergy, instead of as making up the essential people-like character of the Church. We need to declericalize the image of the Church and recatholicize the image of the laity, if the Church is to have any outward thrust.

"In the New Testament doing is usually subsidiary to being. What the laity *are* matters more than what they *do*. Their visible existence as the people of God is more important than anything else. To be a real layperson in the world means the renunciation of all cloisters of escape and all gothic porches for hiding in from unfriendly storms. Every layperson is, so to speak, a St. Christopher, a Christ-bearer, in so far as he [or she] fulfills a secular vocation as a Christian. He [or she] is one grain of that salt, one particle of that light, which is the Church in its relation to the world. By

45

being [this, she or he] embodies the Church's outward thrust. By confessing Christ before [people] through an open life he [or she] is part of the Christian mission."
—**Douglas Webster**[29]

CONGREGATIONAL LIFE-STYLES

1. "With regard to its present life-styles: the congregation must recognize its own participation in a world which continues to reject its king, and *bring its own practices and activities continually before God, in repentance and humility* and with openness to correction and change.

2. "With regard to relationship to the community: the congregation must *inquire from and listen to persons in all areas of community life*—becoming aware of hurt, injustice and deprivation of dignity and self-reliance—and bring these concerns into their life together before the word of God, and follow God's leading in meeting the issues. The congregation must also bring the unbeliever and antagonist into its corporate life to hear and learn through them.

3. "With regard to discerning God's work beyond the limits of the organized church: the members of the congregation must seek to discern God's presence in the world, confronting that which oppresses, exploits or enslaves. They should *respond creatively to the cry for liberation and human development* from the Third World, and from groups in their own country and town. They should *seek to enter into this action of God along with persons of all faiths and of no faith* who are committed to that which expresses God's will and rule in human life, acknowledging that none of us is complete without [our neighbor].

4. "With regard to educating its members for decisive action in God's mission: the congregation should *pursue those forms of education which grow out of and make effective its carrying out of its mission.* Unrelated to mission, church education becomes irrelevant and hypocritical.

5. "With regard to sustaining and renewing the freshness and strength of its members: the congregation should *multiply channels of the creative and redeeming love of*

God, such as prayer fellowships, Bible study groups, sensitivity groups, retreats, etc., so that the healing and growth of each person may stem from and be expressed in a relationship of trust and respect."—**E. H. Johnson**[30]

STUDY QUESTIONS

1. Reread E. H. Johnson's "Missional Vision." Does he describe your church? What is one way you individually can change it? If he does not describe your church write a paragraph describing the vision and action of your church engaging in mission.

2. Ask five people, youth and adults, in your church to give you one illustration from your own church in regard to Johnson's five points on "Congregational Life-styles." What is your church's strength in these five points? What are its weaknesses? What next step can you take to improve, to raise the consciousness of people, to enter into action with persons of other denominations or other faiths?

2
mission education

Some authors place mission into the context of the total educational ministry of the local church. Mission and education inform each other.

A NEW ERA IN EDUCATION FOR MISSION

"Since every church everywhere is living in a mission situation, the main task in education for mission must be to assist, enable, encourage the churches in every situation, country and continent to see and fulfill their mission. We cannot any longer divide 'foreign mission' and 'home mission,' because the mission of the church is one and must be seen in one perspective. The main task of all mission education is to help the whole church, as the people of God, to be a witnessing community here and now—and in all places.

"To 'see mission whole,' the most important thing is not to educate the specialists and missionaries but the whole church: each congregation, the whole people, the *laos* of God, for witness and mission. All training of laity should have this focus.

" 'Seeing mission whole' points to the need to see mission in relation to all realms of life and all aspects of human nature. In the proclamation of the Gospel there is no such thing as 'pure preaching.' The Good News, and therefore the mission, has always involved the whole of life. Those involved in mission necessarily tackle questions of race, justice, development. The issues may change but the involvement with the whole of life is true to the Bible. The question of what 'salvation' means when dealing with these issues is constantly before us.

"If mission is really taught 'seeing mission whole,' being involved in the Christian witness everywhere and in all realms of life, in most burning issues of today's world, it certainly could become one of the most interesting subjects."—**Inga-Brita Casteren**[31]

EDUCATION FOR MISSION

"Education for mission indicates that the objective of this special area of the church's educational responsibility is to help persons respond in faith and love to God through Jesus Christ by fulfilling their discipleship in the Christian mission. As Christians, each of us should understand Christ's mission as it applies to us and to the whole world. We are called to involve ourselves in mission where we live and, as much as possible, in every other part of the world. What we learn about the mission of the church elsewhere will instruct us in our own Christian duty. Our involvement in mission in our own community will lead us to a concern for the mission everywhere.

"An important part of education for mission must be education about missions—about the projects and programs by which the churches seek to fulfill their responsibility at home and around the world. The churches have developed an extensive missionary program.

"This work needs the support of Christian people in terms of intelligent understanding, prayer, personnel and money. Such support grows out of effective education and motivation. At this point, education and promotion are closely allied.

"Attention to specific missionary projects and activities should always be related to the total Christian mission. An effective missionary education program will lead persons beyond an interest in one area or one kind of work to and awareness of world mission strategy. It will guide them to understand the transitions occurring in missionary work. Church members, for example, who for years have supported a favorite school in Malaya, will need to understand why the church may have closed it or turned it over to government control. Those whose favorite missionary may have been transferred from one country to another, or may even have been left at home without a new assignment, must see the issues that brought about such a decision by the board of missions or the overseas church. In all possible ways, church members need an education that helps them respond affirmatively, in attitude and action, to the mission's dynamic nature. . . .

"There are many churches where facilities are ideal, where materials are excellent, where teachers are well-trained, but where missionary zeal and vision are absent. Such situations fall short of the Christian standard. They show unmistakably that, without clear attention by leaders and program, the missionary duty of the Christian recedes into vague and indifferent response.

"If education for mission is to be effective, certain persons must assume it as their chief responsibility. It is the concern of all Christians, and it should be planned to involve as many people as possible, but a core of devoted, trained leaders must take the initiative. Every function of the church needs its leaders. In the New Testament church, Paul described this division of function, suggesting that Christ's gifts were that 'some should be apostles, some prophets, some evangelists, some pastors and teachers.' In a twentieth century congregation, some must be leaders in mission and education for mission.

"An adequate program of Christian education also requires periods of special concentration when the mission of the church is brought into sharp focus for the congregation, or any of its groups. Such learning experiences are frequently based on annual themes, selected interdenominationally and supported by interdenominationally published materials. The themes create an opportunity for congregations of many denominations to pursue the same area of study and to unite in occasions of leadership development and community activity.

MISSION EDUCATION

"In addition to organized efforts in education for mission, a church can always keep the missionary motive of its work before its members by exhibits, displays, book tables and special notices. Churches should use more imagination in focusing attention on some special interest or occasion by an attractive exhibit. They are often outdone by public schools, libraries or other secular institutions. The life and work of the church around the world provides an excellent subject for such indirect teaching. 'A picture is worth a thousand words,' but only if it is placed where it can be seen.

"Whether people are reading more or less since the advent of television, one thing cannot be denied—the publishing of books continues to increase. Someone buys books, and of all those who ought to keep abreast of the times, Christian people should. One unlimited opportunity to accomplish education for mission is to encourage people to read the publications made available to them on the missionary work of the church.

"To sum up, education for mission is integral to the structure of every church. It must be provided for. It should be a concern of the minister and the church's official council. It should be a special interest of the church's board or committee on Christian education. It should be the chief responsibility of a special group of informed and dedicated leaders."—**J. Allan Ranck** [32]

EDUCATING THE CONGREGATION FOR MISSION

"Every congregation must be provided with clear opportunities to understand and undertake the missionary obligations of the church. This is the duty of missionary education—education for mission.

"Education for mission is the obligation of the congregation's administrative council or session, under the leadership of the minister. It deserves and requires no less than the authority and concern of the official body that supervises the total program of the church. Consequently, this council or session should oversee the assignment to leaders and committees of responsibility for education for mission. It should provide sufficient financial resources in the church's budget for an effective missionary education program. During specific activities in the program, the official board should use its influence to encourage their success.

"The congregation will probably have a committee or board of Christian education to which falls responsibility for the total educational program of the church. Its members will represent all the age-groups and educational activities of the church. In this Christian education committee lies a large part of the responsibility for the missionary education effort.

"Many churches form a committee specifically for missionary education, usually as a sub-committee of the official board or of the Christian education committee. Its membership and duties depend on the congregation's organization. This committee should include representatives of all groups that have an interest in or responsibility for missionary education—church school, women's society, men's organization, youth groups, missions or outreach commission, deacons. It should coordinate all the activities carried on in a program of education for mission. Obviously, its members should be persons who can devote enough time to guarantee the congregation an effective program.

"We need to be aware of a danger in establishing this special committee. It should not lead anyone to conclude that its program belongs to a few individuals or the groups they represent. The mission of the church includes every Christian. Means should be found to involve every church member in it. Education for mission is essential for everyone, because participation in the Christian mission is essential for every one.

"In some churches in the past, the mission of the church was considered an interest of women alone. The men kept their hands off and the women did a work that won praise and admiration. In today's world, however, the mission is hampered by such an allocation of responsibility. Our congregation's activities in education for mission should be an integral part of the total education and interpretation program of the church, for the participation of the entire membership."—**J. Allan Ranck** [33]

HELPING THE CONGREGATION ENGAGE IN MISSION

"There is a new awareness today of the need to spread the gospel into the systems which dominate our lives: economic systems which predetermine that a few will be very rich while most people in the world will be very poor; cultural systems which promote racial fears and institutionalize those fears into unfair housing, employment, legal, and other practices; power systems which control war and peace, education, health services, information available to the public, as well as political freedom. Mission is being conceived systemically—the systems of [people] are the new frontiers of mission. The goal is to humanize these systems, which so often depersonalize and exploit persons, into structures which fulfill persons. This understanding of mission has many implications for the local congregation.

"Characteristics of a Congregation Engaged in Changing Oppressive Systems

"From research studies and wide experience in community organization and social change, it has been found that certain qualities and skills are necessary for a congregation to be able to engage successfully in systems change.

"1. *Sensitivity to and solidarity with the victims of oppression.* As Jesus identified with the outcasts and victims of his day, so the local congregation must identify with the victims of oppressive systems and structures today, in the community, the nation, and in other nations. This means victims of urbanization, poor housing, inadequate education, unemployment, inadequate health services, poverty, war.

"2. Analytical and diagnostic skills. When congregations fail in mission, it is usually because too little time has been spent in careful analysis of community and/or world problems. This includes analysis of power structures. Best results occur when clergy and lay persons receive training together in analysis and diagnosis of community issues.

"3. Strategy planning and evaluation skills. Lay and clergy alike need increased skills in moving society toward the realization of true community, including:

"a. Participatory skills for exercising present possibilities for decision-making within existing institutions to make them more just, inclusive, open.

"b. Controlling skills to gain decision-making influence in any arena or system which affects their lives.

"c. Confronting skills to press systems from outside because of their unwillingness or inability to change from within.

"Steps a Congregation Can Take to Equip Itself for Mission

"1. Bring together small teams of lay people to plan together for mission. Study *Listening to Lay People* to discover ways to be in mission in occupational, political, social and other in-the-world relationships and responsibilities. This is the beginning of a mission to institutions.

"2. Engage the Council on Ministries in a study of church and community. This should provide you with many possibilities for mission.

"3. Join with other congregations and organizations in special ministries regarding your community's youth, women, the elderly, racial and ethnic minorities, education and literacy, employment and economic development, law-order-and-justice, nutrition, hunger, health services, family-life services, drugs, community services such as sewage disposal, recreation and parks, public transportation, people with a highly mobile-life-style, and others not reached by the church who need the care, opportunities for growth in self-fulfillment, and faith which the church provides.

"4. Provide intensive training of lay-clergy teams. Use outside consultants such as the Action Training Coalition or the Urban Consultation Team. Or use a process guide for social change.

"5. Hold a community-wide think-tank conference to consider the future of your community in 2023. Bring together business [people], builders, editors, homeowners, students, politicians, planners, as well as churches. Create a model of the kind of community people would like to have in 2023."—**Charles H. Ellzey and Paul M. Dietterich** [34]

MISSION: THE OBEDIENT NUCLEUS

" 'The disciplined fellowship of religious societies is the real clue to evangelical religion.' (Max Warren)

"That sentence is not a description of an historical episode but the statement of an abiding principle. It is a principle which was first enunciated by the prophets of Israel as part of their critique of both the Church and the nation of their day. It is the principle of the obedient nucleus. The covenant which God made with Abraham conferred great privilege and great responsibility upon Israel as a whole. But it was the seven thousand who did not bow the knee to Baal, the faithful remnant, the suffering servant, which actually responded and rose up to discharge God's purpose on behalf of the whole people.

"However true it may be theologically that the whole Church is to be the servant of God and the Body of Christ in the world, in practice there has always been an obedient nucleus which carried the responsibility on behalf of the whole Church in a particular direction. For example, the whole Christian community ought to have been concerned in the matter of slavery in the eighteenth and nineteenth centuries; but in fact it was through the obedience of the Clapham Sect and other groups that the Church made its witness and exercised its healing ministry on that issue. It is worth remembering that the obedient nucleus, at least in its early days, has always seemed to be a lunatic fringe.

"So also the Mission to the world is the primary task of the whole Church; yet throughout its history all the great periods of advance have been due to the response of an obedient nucleus. This has consisted for the most part of ordinary church members, yet there is no evidence that at any time were *all* church members equally obedient. Central and Northern Europe was evangelized from the sixth to the twelfth centuries by individual wanderers for Christ, such as Columban, Gall, Boniface, Anskar and the small monastic groups which followed them.

"Do the circumstances of our own day constitute a sound reason for reversing this principle of the obedient and representative nucleus which has proved its validity through so centuries of sacred history?"—**John V. Taylor**[35]

STUDY QUESTIONS

1. List ten words defining mission. Check these with a person in another age group in your church. Then write a paragraph together defining mission.

2. If you are working on this book in a group ask 12 persons to each take one month and write one way your church could be educated for mission during that month. Put it together on newsprint; locate omissions and repetitions. Revise and use a possible plan for education for mission in your church.

3. Look at the five steps Ellzey and Dietterich suggest for a congregation equipping itself for mission. Which one would be important for your church to tackle? Take some responsibility for making the next step.

4. Do you see everything in your church as mission or is mission a unique part of the church program? If it is unique, what is its uniqueness and *how* does it function in a local church?

SECTION III

mission
happening

1
planning
and structure

Based on the assumption that "mission" is a vital and integral part of the life of any local church, mission activities must be seen as a normal part of the life-pattern of a parish. In addition to specific programs or projects which can be labeled "mission," there is also, perhaps even of greater significance, the mood or atmosphere of mission which should permeate all activities.

Earlier, mission was based solidly on the "Great Commission" and was placed before church members by quoting Matthew 28:19—"Go, then, to all peoples everywhere and make them my disciples: baptize them in the name of the Father and of the Son and of the Holy Spirit" (TEV). Or, Acts 1:8—"You will be witnesses for me in Jerusalem, in all of Judea and Samaria, and to the ends of the earth" (TEV.)[36] As useful, instructive and compelling as such quotes may be, people in the 1970s are not responding as formerly to such mandates.

A firmer base of mission involvement and action is to begin with God. God is disclosed to us in a manner that calls forth a natural reply. God loves; we love. God forgives; we forgive. God cares; we care. God gives; we give. God serves; we serve. God our Father, revealed in Jesus Christ, is the motive, the drive, the reason, the inspiration, even the content of our mission. Martin Luther said it this way:

> I believe that Jesus Christ . . . is my Lord.
> He has redeemed me,
> a lost and condemned person,

saved me at great cost
from sin, death . . .
not with silver or gold,
but with his holy and precious blood
and his innocent suffering and death.
All this he has done that I may be his own,
live under him in his kingdom,
and serve him.[37]

This is to say that the mission of God's people flows from the nature of our God. We are not *commanded* to witness; we gladly *share* the good news. We are not living by a *law*; we are giving our "yes" to God's *love*. Legalism does not lead to mission, only to conformity. The Christian mission is a happy affirmation of God and of our servanthood.

This mood or spirit shapes the life-style of the local church. Mission infuses itself into the web of congregational activities. At each place, the mission dimension should be discerned. Think of the typical activities of the local church and you outline where mission should be.

• *Preaching.* Mood here is most important; a sermon need not be explicitly "mission" each week, but implicitly it has to be, for that is what we are about. Yet beyond mood there is a place and need for specific "mission sermons." Where a visiting missionary, either overseas or national in focus, is available, the sermon can be an exciting mix of "mission report" and scriptural content. The local pastor is not excused from his or her own mission sermon by using a missionary; happily blessed is a local church where the residing minister preaches mission.

• *Worship.* Corporate worship is a major aspect of the local church's life. How can it reflect mission? Worship resources from overseas churches, including music, can deepen awareness of the world-wide church. The increased variety in congregational worship suggests that litanies, liturgies, responses, prayers, art forms and other devotional tools can be brought in from other lands, other communions, other languages. Christians of other traditions and other places can contribute to us.

• *Teaching.* The various educational endeavors of the local church can all be mission education opportunities. In significant ways, mission concepts and learnings are creatively presented in the parish education curriculum of most denominations; the local church needs to understand these, encourage their fulfillment and assist the teacher or class in expanding this experience. Consultation with demoninational education leaders will show how and where mission education is wisely included in resources already in use. Organizational activities—women, men, couples, youth, etc.—present excellent occasions for programs, projects, studies or special events to be bent toward mission education.

• *Fellowship.* "Family Nights" or fellowship events or refreshments or cottage meetings can be pleasant times for reminding members of the mission of the church. Food, games, entertainment and music can widen interests and awareness. The local church cannot honestly be only focused upon itself; concern and attention needs to be extended "to the ends of the earth."

• *Service.* The care and nurture of the local household of faith is an obvious task of a local church; there are numerous methods for serving both members and local persons in need. Mission reminds us that service is also for those beyond our immediate vision: the hurt in city and farm; the addict; the victim of drought, flood or earthquake; the handicapped; blind; deaf. Church World Service, Lutheran World Relief, Catholic Overseas Relief represent organized ways for goods and funds to touch the world's pain. We should support them to the fullest. Consultation with denominational leaders will show other ways for direct service or indirect service by influencing government and business. Our hand and voice must be raised in the service of fellow humans.

MISSION STRUCTURE

In the deepest sense, local church mission education is the heart of being and doing. This is the area of life that shows what is central and determinative for the congregation. It is mission education that says to us and to others that Christ is the center of our fellowship, that sharing him is the key to our calling, that here is how and where we differ from community or social organizations and clubs.

Where does mission education reside in the structure of the local church? There is no one answer for everyone, for every local church. The size of the local church, the number and quality of leaders, the size and character of the local community, the number and relationship of other Christian communions, the economic and social dimensions of the community, the history of involvement in mission by the local church, all these, and other factors, give uniqueness to the local structure for mission education. The local church will establish its own structure and pattern.

The following factors should be considered as a given local church plans for its mission education structure.

What suggestions are offered by denominational agencies for local structure? Such suggestions would not be blueprints to be followed without questioning, without modifying for the given local situation. Denominational suggestions can offer meaningful ties with cooperating churches and with resources and leadership beyond the local, a consciousness of a wider fellowship and helpful ideas for local consideration.

The local church should lodge mission education somewhere in its structure. Mission education should not be an option; it should be a required function of the local church. Some structure, sub-structure or individual, should be provided with official status for accomplishing mission education in the local church. Accountability needs to be determined. Visibility of mission education should be assured. To see mission education as everyone's task or failing to assign the job to someone suggests that it will be lost in the total effort or will not adequately be faced.

Determined by local church size, priorities, characteristics, leadership, etc., mission education could be structured from the following possible options.

(a) *A committee on mission education.* A group would be charged with the task of mission education. It might be called a committee, a task force, a commission, a board. It might be composed of three persons or 20 persons. This group would have the responsibility for seeing that mission education permeates the life of the local church. It would undertake certain activities itself; it would work through other groups or program units wherever feasible.

(b) *A subcommittee on mission education.* Again, this is a group charged with the mission education job. Depending upon local church practice or structure, such a subcommittee would be an outgrowth of a larger segment of the local church program, related to the Christian education committee (this would underscore the educational task), or related to the stewardship committee (this would tie mission to the financial support system), or related to an outreach commission or some other umbrella board.

(c) *A person assigned as mission interpreter, coordinator or expediter.* One individual is given the task of overseeing the mission education or mission consciousness of the local church. If the membership is small, if the insight to the job is not large, if a *beginning* is better than nothing, then one person might be enough. This coordinator, even more than a group, must have some commitment to mission, wisdom to move among and with other structures in the local church, a low profile to ward off obnoxiousness and an ability to generate enthusiasm.

The ideas for being and doing, for making mission happen in *your* local church, can be meaningful and useful only as they fit into your developing local patterns. Activities, no matter how interesting and appealing, have to blend into your life-style as a local church. Busyness, in and of itself, is totally unacceptable today. Activism demands knowing "who you are" and "where you are going."

PLANNING PROCESS

After years of criticism and denunciation, the local church has come back strong as the *center* of Christian activity.

With all the inherent weaknesses portrayed through sociological analysis, the local parish continues to represent the church's best possibility. It is in the local situation that meaningful fellowship can exist, that lives can be changed, that minds can study and grow, that service seems possible, that outreach is a viable option.

With renewed energy and potential, the local church is seeking ways to be more effective, to conduct its life more wisely. One of the better methods to come into wide use is "planning"—a concept utilized broadly in business and government.

Planning asks the local church to examine itself carefully and to articulate its objectives. All too often the local church does not see itself fully: what is the nature of the membership, what is the nature of the community, what are the strengths and weaknesses of each, where do needs call for action? Rather than following program patterns developed 20 or 30 years before, no matter how dynamic they might have been earlier, the local church must re-state its goals so that a life-style for *today* can emerge.

The examination of the local church's situation and its statement of purpose, both of which can lead to a renewal of its programmatic task, are the products of the planning process. This procedure holds such great potential for the local church that it is suggested as essential for establishing the climate for "making mission happen."

Every local church seeking to renew or recast itself can obtain helpful guidance from its denominational leadership. "Church planning" by any name is almost certainly a part of the service available to the local church from the denomination. A contact to the agency related to parish life should bring valuable assistance.

Few national denominational headquarters will submit packages for local church swallowing. It can't be done today! The local church will have to begin with basics (theology and faith-statements), from which it will create its own expression of Christian fellowship, service and witness. This mind-stretching, heartrending process is the requirement

63

for today and the future. Local churches must identify themselves ("Who are we?" "What is the church in this place now?") and determine their program ("What do we do?" "What is our task here and now?"). The planning process of carefully articulating objectives, and then working out activities for fulfilling such, needs to become the pattern for local church operations as it is at denominational offices.

Among the books which have been found beneficial in rejuvenating congregations are Douglas Johnson's *Managing Change in the Church* (New York: Friendship Press, 1974) and *Planning for Ministries 1973 and Beyond* (Council on Ministries, The United Methodist Church, 601 West Riverview Avenue, Dayton, Ohio 45406).

Persons interested in pursuing long-range planning further will find Lyle Schaller's *The Impact of the Future* stimulating and exciting (Nashville: Abingdon Press, 1969). The book's subtitle *Trends Affecting the Church of Tomorrow* helps to capture it significance.

PARISH RENEWAL

The church book market has been flooded with volumes analyzing and prescribing for the local church's life and fate. It is good: the local church needs all the assistance available to reexamine its situation and opportunities. The critical evaluations of the late 50s and early 60s have been, happily, replaced by constructive suggestions.

Readers are urged to dig into the literature describing and suggesting plans and programs for parish renewal. One will hardly "follow" any authority or recommendation fully or exclusively, but stimulation and inspiration from numerous sources could reshape your ideas. One good place to begin —and then move on to other authors or schemes—is *The Base Church,* a book by Charles M. Olsen (Atlanta: Forum House, 1973). Olsen's concept of small—"base"—groups, and their place in the life of the church, will click imaginations. Using his references as a platform, you can pursue other ideas that could ignite your local church. The small group, or cell, with its strong biblical association, represents not only a developing pattern of church activities but addresses creatively the style of corporate life which appears to be both accepted and effective in alive congregations.

STOP: EVALUATE

The following passage, reprinted from *The Interpreter,* can help you evaluate your mission education program. When you come to the questions, answer each of them with one of four answers: Yes, No, Partly, and Don't Know.

"On occasion we need to take time to evaluate our missionary education program. Learning from mistakes and failures of the past, we may be more effective in the future.

"Sincere evaluation of the missionary education program is a problem. We avoid such evaluation by assuming people automatically incorporate new learnings in their lives and by assuming that programs cannot be improved very much even if evaluated.

"Too often programs are labeled as good or bad by one person or by those who plan them. Both learners and administrators must cooperate in organized evaluation.

"Any program of education for mission should include time for evaluation by the participants. It is a way to find out if a person or group accomplished what was initially set as a goal. To make evaluation possible the goals must be known in advance. Without evaluation, goals are lost, programs tend to be purposeless, patterns are unchanged, inappropriate procedures become habitual and progress cannot be measured. Evaluation increases awareness of goals and results and enables adjustment of programs to meet needs that participants recognize."

1. Do we have a committee or task force on education for mission?

2. Does it meet, plan, make proposals and serve as an advocate for mission in the church?

3. Is the committee representative of the church?

4. Does our church engage in long-range planning?

5. Have we developed an opportunity for our people to

acquire a general knowledge of mission history and outstanding missionary personalities throughout the centuries?

6. Have we provided opportunity for our people to develop an appreciation for and knowledge of the biblical basis of mission?

7. Do we conduct an annual school of mission for all age groups?

8. Do we have a mission emphasis in vacation church school?

9. Are we helping our congregation to see the role of our denomination in the total scope of world-wide mission?

10. Do we have membership classes or instruction for new members? Do we include the importance of mission?

11. Are we challenging our people and giving them opportunities for response to mission?

12. Do we have a planned program for teaching mission throughout our total church program?

13. Do we have a growing mission section in our audiovisual library and do we encourage its use?

14. Do we have a growing mission section in our church library?

15. Do we project mission in an attractive way through bulletin board displays and printed messages?

16. Do we keep people informed about the church of Christ in the world-wide scene?

17. Do we have systematic training in giving to mission through our church school and church?

18. Is our church moving toward the ideal of giving as much for others as is spent on itself?

19. Does our church highlight news of mission efforts each week in our bulletin or weekly newsletter?

20. Is our congregation informed of our progress in mission giving, at least monthly?

21. Are prayers for specific missionaries, mission stations and projects a part of each worship service?

22. Are periodicals which interpret the mission program in the homes of our members?

"You may add questions to this evaluation. As a result of

this kind of self-study, you may wish to make changes in your mission education plans." [38]

STUDY QUESTIONS

1. "If the church is not local, it's not the church; if the church is only local, neither is it the church." Do you agree or not? Why or why not? In what ways can the local church be "in mission"?

2. Where does "mission education" belong in the life and activities of the local church?

3. What is the practical accent sounded for the local church in the title of this book? What problem arises from the title?

4. Use your calendar of education for mission as suggested in the previous section and check it against the several suggestions in this whole section of the book. Revise if needed.

5. If you are studying this book in a group invite the committee or task force or board responsible for mission education in your church to meet with your group for one session. Discuss the learnings in your group and ways you might work together to carry out some of the suggestions this group has developed.

2
happenings

This chapter is a listing of "mission happenings" which could occur in your local church and community. How can the idea be wisely adapted to your situation? What other idea does this suggest?

MAKE IT PERSONS

1. *Missionary Visit.* Invite a missionary home on furlough to your church. Give a wide exposure: worship, Sunday church school, meet with local church leaders, have an "open house" or reception, visit the ill and shut-ins, get a spot on the local radio or TV "talk show" or arrange for a missionary to record a series of media devotions for later airing or be a speaker at a civic club or at school classes. Invite other churches to share in the events.

2. *Mission Speaker.* Encourage local church organizations to have mission speakers in their programming. Beyond the missionary on furlough, remember the national mission worker not far away who is addressing local mission situations. A member of a denominational mission board could be invited to share his/her insight from meetings and contacts. Jurisdictional unit staff members have experience in the wider mission outreach of the denomination; beyond asking such persons to "do their thing" for the local church, stretch them and yourself by asking them to help you grow in mission, to relate to you the mission of the church as their eyes see it from place to place.

3. *Former Missionaries.* Most denominations have a list or can supply the information as to where retired missionaries

live. Such persons often represent a lifetime of service in mission to other people. As is being demonstrated almost daily, the "senior citizen" has much to offer the rest of society and should not be put out to pasture. The insights into people and cultures, into diverse issues which belong to a servant of the Lord after years of dedication, can be shared in a fresh way.

4. *Overseas National.* Invite an overseas national to your church; follow the same pattern of opportunities listed for a missionary visitor. Many nationals are studying at colleges and universities; be considerate in your invitation. Do not unduly interfere with their primary task of education. Some students represent an elite background; care needs to be taken in selecting such speakers. Request for funds or support should be referred to denominational mission agencies.

5. *Travel.* Individuals or groups can learn through travel experiences. Many denominations conduct overseas "interpretation through travel" or seminars for first-hand exposure to other cultures, peoples, churches. Such contact with the "first-century Christianity" of the church overseas can be a tremendous mission education. The "story" seen and heard should be shared meaningfully back home, not alone with one local church, but with neighboring churches and regional jurisdictions. Excursions to national mission situations or programs, to colleges, homes for aged or children, inner city agencies or parishes, etc. can be developed for weekends or summer "travel caravans." Individuals or groups can participate in "work camp" experiences, both in North America and overseas.

6. *Traveling Sales Persons.* The mobility of North American people is measured in many ways. Consider the traveling sales person or executive: many have territories which could put them into face-to-face contact with national mission projects, or even international efforts. Encourage such persons to visit, when "on the road," these mission situations and then to report back. The person will grow and the local church will widen its perspective.

EVENT CENTERED

1. *School of Mission.* An educational/interpretative event, half-a-day, a full-day, a series of evenings over several weeks, a special session in the Sunday church school or youth fellowship or women's organization. The event or series can be intergenerational, interdenomiational, community-wide. Any and all types of educational processes can and should be used: lectures, audio-visuals, missionary speaker, book reviews, map displays, art exhibits, etc.

2. *Mission Weekend.* Plan a whole weekend around mission themes. The central event, congregational worship, can include the sermon, music, banners, etc. on a mission focus. The Sunday church school, including opportunities for adults, can place emphasis on mission education using either Friendship Press or denominational resources. There could be small Bible study cells; all might study the same passage, or explore separate selections for sharing. A family evening or festival could unite the parish in fellowship.

3. *Mission Retreat.* Any group of members, youth or adults, could gather at an appropiate location for a weekend retreat. Speakers, study materials, action programs and activities can be tied together on a mission issue or theme or country. Foods and games and songs and study could be intertwined into an in-depth approach. Adults might approach a controversial or probing subject best when a whole weekend is available rather than shorter periods of time. Use of speakers, films, books could lead toward deeper understandings.

4. *Family Night.* Combine food, fun, fellowship, learning with a mission emphasis. Plan carefully each part of the evening; include activities and interests for every age group. Remember the "singles" and others not normally included in "family" arrangements. The program format could take the shape of a *Mission Fair,* with booths and displays.

5. *Mission Sunday.* Plan an annual "Mission Sunday" for your local church. Let it be more than an invited preacher

for the morning. Involve as many members as possible. Beyond special attention at Sunday worship (more than just a mission speaker), let the Sunday church school and other events reflect the emphasis of the day.

6. *Fifth Sunday for Mission.* Each year has four months with five Sundays. Put a mission emphasis on that fifth Sunday. Let the preacher's theme be on mission. Develop displays, special lessons in the Sunday church school, a potluck meal. Take a special offering and give to general mission effort or a special project.

7. *Progressive Dinner.* Plan a social or fellowship event designed to widen appreciation for other cultures. Let each "course" be characteristic of a different area of the world; let the background music be appropiate. Venturesome hosts might even dress for their area! Entertainment might be songs from the areas, or explanations of local customs.

8. *Dialogue Sermon.* Have a local church member share in a dialogue sermon with the pastor; or have the pastor or lay member similarly share with a visiting mission speaker. Congregational attention can be sharpened up by this method; extremely relevant questions can be raised and discussed. Use this pattern in other speaking situations.

9. *Ecumenical Round-Robin.* Have well-informed mission persons from various communions share in programs or events in other churches. It will become amazing how much work we do *together* overseas or in certain projects at home. Insights and learnings gleaned from mission contacts or persons can inspire others beside the member church. Ecumenical projects, relationships or institutions around the world tie local churches together; those common involvements should enlarge and strengthen our understanding of the "one church." The *Mission Fair* idea might fit well into an interchurch event, with each local church developing a booth or pavilion.

VISUAL ATTRACTION

1. *Bulletin Board.* Most local churches have a bulletin board for posting notices, posters and clippings. Use it

for "mission items." Mount on color paper for eye-focus. Or, develop a section of the board for mission items, changing it every week or so for freshness. A "mission picture" of the week or month could be posted; pictures can be cut from magazines or books.

2. *Mission Bulletin Board.* If the local church is large enough, or interested/aggressive enough, devote an entire bulletin board to mission. Put it in a prominent location; keep changing the material for freshness and interest. A good way to keep the subject before the eye of the congregation.

3. *Posters.* Mission posters designed for a special emphasis or program can be modified or redesigned for continued use. Here is a project for a youth group: design mission posters for the local church or for some special event. Poster-making can be a project for a "family night"—for all ages. Posters can be accumulated over a period of time and made into an art exhibit for display in the local church, library and bank or department store window.

4. *Displays.* Using pictures, artifacts or other objects develop an educational display. This can be related to an issue (race relations) or to a country (India) or to a project (inner city agency).

5. *Art Exhibits.* A variety of art is available for creative use in the local church. Some denominations have traveling art exhibits of genuine, authentic art executed by Christian artists around the world. These expressions of the Christian faith and biblical themes can represent an important witness to us from the Third World; it is one dimension of "mission to six continents." Friendship Press has published several art portfolios which provide reproductions for display. Many items of art have been used in filmstrips and can be utilized in an art exhibit. Collection of magazine covers or pictures or art illustrations can provide a source worthy of exhibiting.

6. *Banners.* Flannel and other cloth banners have become popular in many local churches. Where such are being designed and made, see if one or more could be done on a

mission theme. These might be made especially for a mission event and then retained for regular use by the church.

TELLING IT

1. *Parish Bulletin*. It is the rare local church which does not have a Sunday worship bulletin or program sheet. Selected quotes can be inserted in the announcement section; prayer requests can be listed; mission news items can be shared.

2. *Parish Paper*. Many local churches have a parish newspaper. See that a mission column is started, or intersperse items. Such a paper can be an important channel for mission information and education.

3. *Local Newspaper*. Editors of local newspapers will use mission related news items, especially when the story can be related to a local church, event or person. Since the local church is related to far-flung efforts toward relieving pain, suffering and injustice, prepare news items indicating how the local church is serving or helping in the midst of a crisis or emergency. When a missionary or national or church worker from beyond your community visits, arrange for an interview with the local press. Even better, if you have a capable writer in your membership have her/him prepare something for submission to the press.

AN IDEA OR TWO

1. *Missionaries as "Staff."* When local churches share in supporting a missionary, national or overseas, an opportunity is presented to keep the vision before the members. Whenever and however (Sunday bulletin, letterhead, etc.), the missionary can be listed as part of the "staff." At the annual congregational meeting, an official written report from the staff missionary can be included along with all other reports.

2. *Mission Telephone Calls*. As part of a worship service, banquet program or study session, place a long distance phone call and speak with a mission person. The cost for an overseas call is not necessarily prohibitive. Plan the call

well so that each minute is effectively used, get input which is uniquely related to the distant speaker and not as easily supplied locally. Special equipment is available to amplify the call, or play it through the public address system.

3. *Church Festivals related to Mission*. Plan a Christmas or Easter service or party with customs and experiences related to many nations. Food, games, music, dress, stories can come from another environment. It will lead to a sense of oneness which overcomes differences.

4. *Temple Talk*. Have a lay person present each week, every other week or once a month a "Minute for Mission," a "Moment for Mission," a "Three Minute Mission Tour" or a "Temple Talk." Call it by any name, but it is a few minutes of interesting, exciting reporting on what the church is doing in mission. This can be a top-flight addition to the corporate experience of the local church, something to help the mind and heart and pocketbook reach out beyond itself.

5. *Prayer List*. Develop a list of people (missionaries, nationals), churches, institutions, issues, causes. In a systematic way offer intercessory prayer for them. There could be a "mission petition" suggested for each week, to be used by individuals. Another "mission petition" could be included in each Sunday general prayer or in the prayer at organizational meetings. Related picture or article would be placed on the bulletin board or in the Sunday bulletin or in the parish paper. Let prayers be for thanksgiving as well as for requests.

6. *Inserting*. Printed materials from denominational headquarters or other sources, reproduction of missionary letters or quotes from books/magazines, can be used as Sunday bulletin "inserts"—not alone on a Mission Sunday or for a Mission Event, but on any and all Sundays. These same items might also be inserted in the parish paper and mailed to the membership.

7. *Pick-Up Reading*. Most churches have some place where "pick-up reading" materials would be helpful for

the visitor or person waiting. The church lounge table, the church office, the "tract rack" in the church entrance, meeting room, etc. are excellent places for a mission magazine or an attractive book. There are several fine mission books with photographs which would lend themselves to this use.

8. *Mission Names.* Parish house rooms, lounges or the local church itself can be named after mission people or places. "Livingston Hall" can keep the members constantly reminded of a great mission personality. "Uhuru Chapel" blends in an exciting manner the Gospel's gift of freedom with the sense of personal and national freedom in Africa. Names could be changed periodically; they needn't last forever.

9. *Mission Calendar.* Develop a mission calendar on which are listed the dates of famous mission personalities (Carey, Xavier, etc.) and mission events (Edinburgh). Birthdates of denominational missionaries and historic steps in mission can be noted. The calendar can be educational and a constant source of mission information and awareness.

10. *Postage Stamps.* Some stamp collector in the local church might develop a "stamp collection" related to mission. Used or new stamps could be saved or purchased to provide interesting insight and identification with another nation.

11. *Coins and Currency.* Representative coins and paper money can be placed on display, as with postage stamps. New interest and sensitivity can grow from such collections.

12. *Hosting the Missionary.* When the local church receives a mission speaker, hosting such a person can be in itself an effective mission interpretation operation. Assuming it is not too much for the visitor's strength or interest, have him/her stay in a different home each night and take lunch and dinner in different homes—do not always place the visitor in a "mission-minded" family. Try the opposite.

13. *Question/Discussion.* Whatever mission speaker you have, place him/her into a conversational setting for best results. Count on questions and comments to set the agenda and pace. The message content will thus match the interests

of the hearers; human interest insights can be brought home to the local scene more dramatically. "Conversations" with the visiting mission person might well be a pattern for the visit: morning and afternoon talks with women, children and youth; evenings with church leaders, women and men and couples. Many a mission speaker, not exactly at home at a podium, could wow a smaller group in an informal circumstance.

14. *Money.* It is through financial support that members of the local church become personally involved in mission. Tell that story. Indicate how much of the local church budget goes for mission effort. (You might have to dig for this data, but it is available and highly enlightening.) Search out how much and how far your mission dollars go: they could be larger and more effective than imagined! Many local churches do not support adequately or eagerly the mission effort beyond their own local program. Raise sights; encourage vision; illustrate involvements.

15. *Mission Projects.* There are opportunities for the activist to work for mission. Projects for children and women are suggested by Church World Service and Lutheran World Relief. Most mission agencies produce lists of projects for local church fulfillment; write and ask about them. It is always wise to undertake a project having some official approval, else the cost and effort might be unnecessarily wasted. Projects requiring money donations would, of course, be undertaken only after fully meeting the denominational budget quota.

16. *Local Service Club.* Try and get a mission message to the local Lions, Rotary, Kiwanis, etc. The right mission speaker, be it an outsider or a local person with knowledge, could do a real service here. If they use films for programming, an effective mission film could fit in nicely.

CHURCH GROUPS

1. *Parish Organizations.* Every local church has its own style and kind of organizations: youth, men, women, couples, senior citizens, choirs, etc. Whatever the local church

has, and as much as they have, the programming of the groups can include mission thrusts. Book reviews, audio-visuals, speakers, social activities, panel presentations and many methods can be used to present mission material to the members. Friendship Press resources are designed for such structures in the local church.

2. *Sunday Church School.* The leadership of every Sunday church school should be alert to see that every mission contact or emphasis in the denominational educational curriculum is utilized. A mission-minded teacher could find many places for mission illustration and special attention. Someone in the local church could be given the task of feeding mission material to teachers; it means both knowing the curriculum well and having proper mission information to share.

3. *Vacation Church School.* Utilizing denominational mission material, one Pennsylvania congregation prepared a full week's vacation school program on world mission. Creative persons could do this with national missions and mission issues. Friendship Press resources would be helpful here. Denominational VCS material can be adjusted or modified to include a section or unit on mission. If this is done each year, a mission-mindedness will affect both the children and their parents—the whole congregation will be enlivened.

4. *Confirmation Classes.* Confirmation classes, adult membership class or whatever the local church has for youth preparing for membership, offer an opportunity to instill a mission attitude. Faith can be taught and confessed as something to be shared, as the foundation for the world-wide church of Christ. The excitement of new Christians in other cultures can help youth see the dynamic of really accepting their own "new birth."

5. *Study Group.* The small group movement is one of the signs of church renewal. Start such a group around a study of a basic mission text. As they probe the meaning and ways of mission strategy for both national and overseas endeavors, they will find provocative parallels for local mission.

The series of books published by Friendship Press dealing with world studies of churches in mission offer some first-class material for such a cell group. For example, *Stranger in the Land* by Robert Lee (1967) examines five varied, yet typical churches in Japan showing the place of Christianity in Japanese culture. Any group in the local church, seriously interested in broadening its horizons and stretching the local mindset, can profitably engage in mission study.

6. *Work with Key Leaders.* Some materials and programs are meant for the average members, the large numbers. Other items can more effective be presented to key leaders of the local church. See that the denominational mission magazine or annual report is given to the leadership group. Let a given mission visitor spend time with leaders. Develop the "core" of the local church into mission awareness: it will permeate the whole. Leaders to keep in mind: the session, church council or general board; Sunday-school superintendent or director; women's organizations, youth fellowships, worship or music people, etc.

7. *Special Audience.* Members of the local Christian community which might have special interest and receptivity toward the entire area of mission. Too often the aged and shut-ins are forgotten (indeed, this segment of our population represent a mission or issue overlooked much too long). Why not have the visiting mission speaker make a few house calls and share the message? Sometimes the visited can become an effective communication channel, telling many about the special visit they received. Young people might carry a cassette of a mission speaker to the shut-in. The faith and experience of those older can prove highly significant to the younger church member seeking identity.

8. *College Students.* The local church's ministry is addressed to members away from home at college or university (also, those in the armed forces). How can "mission awareness" be maintained for this important group? Send the denomination's mission magazine to the students. Give students a mission book for Christmas; select a book with special relevance for the student reader.

MATERIALS TO USE

1. *Mission File.* Develop a file system into which pictures, clippings, references and other items are placed. Folders can be started on *nations* where your denomination has current work, on *agencies* undertaking mission work, on *areas* of the country or world which deserve your attention, on *issues* or concerns which face your mission program. Besides the obvious church publications, use secular sources for items to be placed in the file: *Time, Newsweek, National Geographic, Saturday Review/World,* newspapers, etc. Place effort on the utilization of the "mission file"— it is not enough to collect the material! Encourage leaders to tap this source for background on a program or topic; have Sunday church school teachers dip into this file; use the material for displays or bulletin boards; use the material in "quotes" for worship bulletins or parish papers.

2. *Parish Library.* The local church could have a library and members could be encouraged to read the books. Such a library ought to have a "mission section"—books and magazines for individual reading and for reference. The books quoted in this volume form a good basic beginning and the Friendship Press Complete Catalog offers more suggestions.

3. *Pictures.* Keep a file of mission pictures (relate to "Visual Attraction," item 1, p. 71). Black and white and full-color pictures of people and situations and projects can be obtained. They will make the story real and exciting. Denominational offices could be of help here. Put a picture on the bulletin board; change it each week or so. What about a mission picture each week or month for every Sunday church school class (or room)? A learning story or a prayer can be associated with the picture. Let the pictures reflect joy and dignity, as well as poverty and suffering.

4. *Audio-Visuals.* Use audio-visuals on mission in the life of the local church. Include in this area: films, filmstrips, slides, recordings, cassettes, etc. Check with your denomination (including regional jurisdictional unit) and see how

films and filmstrips are distributed. Filmstrips worthy of repeated showings should be purchased and placed in a parish library; the same for recordings and cassettes. Films are not just entertainment; they require careful planning so that they are a part of an educational experience. Wise use of an accompanying utilization guide is strongly encouraged.

5. *Music.* Mission-minded persons, or those responsible for mission education, should help a local church keep mission in its music program. Numerous folk-songs relate themes directly or indirectly tied to mission ideas. Use of recordings of music from overseas can be a profound cultural exchange. There are various sources of music from overseas; your denominational mission agency might offer assistance here. Mission hymns might be sung at other meetings than when a missionary is speaking.

6. *Mission Drama.* The drama of mission life and history is most colorful. Some if it has been captured in dramatic skits. Friendship Press has published a sizable list of plays, discussion starters, choral dramas. In addition to being a good source for the local church's actors group, they could be stimulus for a creative writer's own efforts in drama.

7. *Missionary Letters.* Many missionaries write a periodic letter for distribution to family and friends; it is an efficient way to keep in touch with a large number of people. A local church could aid the missionary by offering to mail the letter: maintaining a mailing list, reproducing the letter and mailing it. Those receiving such letters should use them for mission education: post them on the bulletin board, duplicate them for distribution among the local church members, quote from them in the Sunday bulletin or parish paper. When being duplicated, information of a personal nature should be omitted; where policy matters arise, it is helpful to confer with mission agencies. The letters can be filed and used later as resource material. Why not have one or more persons respond to missionary letters. The mails go two ways and a fellowship can be maintained.

3
resources

Here is a running start on resources for your mission education program. Check these out and be on the alert for other items of interest.

SEEING IT

1. *Audio-Visual Resource Guide* (AVRG). An indispensable tool for the entire parish program, this ninth edition of AVRG provides evaluations of more than 2500 films, filmstrips, recordings. Purchase from denominational books stores or audio-visual offices. A wealth of mission AV's are listed in this guide.

2. *Maps.* One of the better ways to develop "global awareness" is the use of maps. Attractively mounted maps might be prominently placed in church lounges or board rooms. Could each classroom, or class area, have a map? Like pictures and clippings, they should be rotated or changed frequently. Map sources: (1) denominational mission agencies might have some, usually with special attention to the denomination's national and world mission activities; (2) Friendship Press has a good selection of maps, including the *Friendship Global Outline Map* and "picture maps" for children's creative touch; and (3) National Geographic Society maps are undoubtedly available from several members of the church. Maps should be used to emphasize the distance and separation between parts of the globe. They are educational tools in learning about the world—we live in a global village, we ought to know the streets!

3. The *electronic media* should not be overlooked as we seek to reach people in the last quarter of the twentieth century. We are glued to the TV! We count on radio for news and entertainment and information. The motion picture has molded our perception of life and death, of good and evil, of what is useful and beautiful. Can the TV "special" (or the regular "news") be utilized to form value judgments and understanding of our world and issues confronting us? The availability of 16mm editions of major motion pictures, along with anticipated video-cassettes of TV programs, will provide ready resources for quality analysis of many issues and situations facing the mission enterprise of the church. Mission education will need to explore ways and means of effectively using these new tools.

4. *Flags of Nations.* A colorful and effective way to identify with other peoples, lands and churches is the display of a nation's flag. Displayed permanently or on special occasions and in an appropriate manner, flags can give reality to new and emerging lands. Various sizes and quality of flags (from all United Nations member countries) can be purchased from Annin and Company, Verona, New Jersey 07044. Write for a current catalog; allow up to three months for delivery of orders.

MAGAZINE RACK

1. *Denominational periodicals* contain important articles and stories worthy of filing. Special attention should be given to mission magazines: exchange between various communions in one community can encourage a mutual sharing of insights.

2. *Current magazines* frequently contain feature articles which can be included in a file system of information. *Time, Newsweek, U.S. News and World Report* and other news publications give analyses of people and places often of more than temporary value. Magazine features also provide in-depth treatment of major issues and nations: Note especially magazines such as *Atlantic Monthly, Holiday, Harpers, National Geographic, Saturday Review/World,* etc.

3. *Context.* This six-page fortnightly "commentary on the interaction of religion and culture" is written by Martin E. Marty of the University of Chicago and *The Christian Century*. It is published by the Thomas More Association, 221 West Madison Avenue, Chicago, Ill., 60606. This is among the best sources of penetrating analysis of current issues. Cost per year: $16.95.

4. *New World Outlook.* This monthly mission magazine serves both the United Methodist and United Presbyterian churches. Focus is both overseas and homeland mission concerns. The magazine is thoughtful and attractive, with very good editorial and news sections. Subscription for one year is $3.00 and can be ordered at 475 Riverside Drive, New York, New York 10027.

5. *World Encounter.* Another worthy mission magazine is published five times a year by the Division for World Mission and Ecumenism, Lutheran Church in America. Themes and subjects of interest beyond its own member readers suggests that this publication can be useful to other denominations. Cost for the year is $1.50; order from 231 Madison Avenue, New York, New York 10016.

6. *World Mission.* This quarterly presents some current Roman Catholic thinking in world missions in an effective manner. Cost is $5.00; order from 366 Fifth Avenue, New York, N.Y. 10001.

7. *CMS Newsletter.* The Church Mission Society related to the Church of England (Anglican) produces a monthly publication. CMS executive John V. Taylor is the articulate author/editor. Perceptive and balanced insights are shared. $2.45 from 175 Waterloo Road, London, SE1 8UU.

8. *World Vision.* This monthly magazine serves the non-denominational, independent mission agency World Vision International, Inc. The promotional and solicitation aspects of the publication, along with materials sent to computerized mailing lists, need not diminish the value of this contact with the evangelical-conservative mission enterprise. The magazine is mailed free. It can be requested from 919 West Huntington Drive, Monrovia, Calif. 91016.

9. *Church Growth Bulletin.* Provocative mission insights from the Bulletin of the School for World Missions and Institute of Church Growth of Fuller Theological Seminary. Subscription includes membership in the Church Growth Book Club, source of many mission books at substantial discounts. The Bulletin is $1.00 per year and ordered at 265 Lytton Avenue, Palo Alto, Calif. 94301. The school and book club are located in South Pasadena.

PEOPLE ORIENTED

1. *Interdenominational Mission Conferences.* Every summer across the United States and Canada, week-long interdenominational mission conferences feature expert resource leaders. Usually based upon interdenominational mission themes or issues, the conferences provide education helps for local church persons charged with mission concern. Denominational agencies can supply information on each summer's program.

2. *Persons.* Ever since Jesus chose his disciples, ever since Calvary shouted the worth of people, ever since mission and missionary became intertwined for the church (albeit, the role of the missionary changes from time to time), ever since we understand our call to be "people for others" —*people* are the focus of the Church of Jesus Christ. It is people—individually and corporately—that are reaching and serving and loving. It is people that can tell the story of mission; we use our imaginations to make mission education personal.

a. *Missionaries* (missioners, fraternal workers, partners, co-workers, or whatever) are among the best "reporters" to the local church. An articulate, excited, informed, committed missionary has ignited the mind and heart of many in a local church. This type of person is still available for our mission education task. Our minds must be stretched to see the possible situations where the missionary can relate to local church and community: Sunday worship, Sunday church school, church organizations, small groups, public school classes, service clubs, radio or TV, home visitations, house "teas" or "coffees" or "receptions," leadership groups. A straight presentation might not be the best method; why not "question periods" or time for real in-depth discussion or dialogue?

b. *Mission Interpreters.* Interested persons are gaining first-hand experience and knowledge of mission efforts. Wide travel on business and pleasure have led active church members to visit people, agencies, churches which give a person-to-person exposure which can be shared significantly with the local church. Denominational offices can supply mission "contact personnel" for such visitors. Many denominational agencies have programs of "mission seminars"—well-planned and well-led group study tours of both national and overseas mission work. Persons sharing these experiences can "report" what they have seen and heard.

PRINT WITH A PLUS

1. *Friendship Press Catalogs.* Each year an annual catalog "Resources for the Church in Mission" is published in January. This publication lists new Friendship Press resources for the study year summer-to-summer, and to be published each spring. A new item necessary for every local church is "The Friendship Press Complete Catalog 1974"; this lists all books, guides, dramas, filmstrips, games, maps, recordings, etc. available from the Press. *The Complete Catalog* is a gold-mine of resources for every local church. These catalogs can be obtained from your denominational publication house, Christian education office or mission agencies; they are also available from Friendship Press, 475 Riverside Drive, New York, New York 10027.

2. *Denominational Material.* Mission and/or education agencies, and sometimes stewardship offices, produce excellent promotional-interpretation-education materials which should become a part of the local church program. Printed folders or flyers, magazines, annual reports, posters, bulletin inserts, audio-visual resources, educational programs are all frequently available for relating to the various

85

aspects of the local church's life. Many of these items should be sampled in the church's filing system. Where close cooperation exists between two or more denominations in one community, it is possible that denominational material can effectively be shared with other denominations: it is a good way to broaden horizons.

3. *Wright Studio.* This independent organization produces interesting and effective resources related to mission education themes. Of special value are those items representative of other cultures and nations. Write directly for this catalog. Address: 5264 Brookville Road, Indianapolis, Ind. 46219.

4. *Background Information.* When studying a specific country, contact all possible sources for useful information. Check with a travel agent or an overseas airline for "travel posters" (a good item for local color). Many nations have tourist offices in New York City and/or other major cities and can supply materials. The official embassies or United Nations delegations in Washington and Ottawa or New York might offer information or resources for an in-depth study of a country.

5. *Public Library.* Examine the local public library to see if it has books and magazines addressing world and current issues. This source has all-too-often been neglected by the local church. Many libraries have recordings and audio-visuals (films, especially) which might be useful in mission education or global awareness. *An opportunity:* Let the local church (or perhaps jointly in an ecumenical venture) purchase mission books and magazines for the public library.

6. *Extra Books.* A subject as important and intriguing as mission has naturally attracted great minds. Not infrequently, such scholars dig deeper than many others are able or interested to go. In selecting quotations for this book, care has been taken to tap resources which could be acceptable and challenging to nonprofessionals.

Two special books are here called to the reader's attention because they offer extraordinary value for the layperson. The first is *Crossroads in Missions,* a "multibook" published by William Carey Library, 533 Hermosa Street, South Pasadena, Calif. 91030. Available at a retail price of $9.95, the volume is a reprint of five choice books published in the 1960s, but out-of-print as single books. The five books are *The Missionary Nature of the Church* by Johannes Blauw, *Missionary, Go Home!* by James A. Scherer, *The Responsible Church and the Foreign Mission* by Peter Beyerhaus and Henry Lefever, *On the Growing Edge of the Church* by T. Watson Street, and *The Missionary Between the Times* by R. Pierce Beaver. None of these are quoted in this present book, but each fits the description of a resource suitable for nonprofessional use in the local church.

The second book represents a more advanced reading assignment for the individual (or study group) wishing to explore deeper the issues facing mission in the church. It is *Eye of the Storm,* edited by Donald McGavran (Waco, Texas: Word Books, 1972). The book examines under the pen of various writers, often in opposition to each other, "the great debate in mission" which still is very much alive. Writers include mainline Protestants, "evangelicals" or conservatives, Roman Catholics and ecumenicals.

The above two books are good collections of mission authorities, easily read without great difficulty. A serious reader can expand his or her knowledge or perception by beginning with these books. A local church wishing members to have access to current mission thinking will place these two volumes in the parish library.

making
mission happen

The foregoing ideas are handles and prodders. They should move you to action and involvement. Here are three frameworks for getting into action.

ECUMENICAL MEASURE

One of the more exciting aspects of the Ecumenical Movement is its origin. The Movement came out of "foreign mission" efforts of the Protestant churches. The first ecumenical conclave was the meeting in Edinburgh, Scotland in 1910; it was in effect an international gathering of mission people. The commission to be about mission was the cause which brought church leaders together to contemplate their oneness.

Facing overwhelming numbers of people, often hostile, missionaries from Europe and North America to the traditional "fields" of Asia, Africa and Latin America joined in fellowship and work. Early missionaries have to a great extent become the common heritage of all: Xavier, Carey, Livingston, Judson, Moffat, Schweitzer, Morrison, Mott. Confessional backgrounds, not ignored, have nevertheless receded from importance as Christians united in mission.

Ecumenical ventures have grown and thrived. In medical work there is Vellore and Ludhiana in India. In educational effort there is International Christian University in Tokyo and Pacific Theological College in Fiji. In mass communications there is the Radio Voice of the Gospel in Addis Ababa. There is the one mission in the United Mission to Nepal. Christians *do* work together effectively in mission.

The scene is the same in North America. In countless local councils of churches, local Christian groups unite in witness and service. Church World Service brings most Protestants into a common effort of world-wide relief. Ministry in the National Parks is conducted jointly. The interchange of ideas and plans and programs mark the cooperative life of denominations.

Mission education is a logical place for ecumenical association in the local community. Lack of leadership, small numbers, few missionaries and nationals, suggest that it is practical to join in facets of mission education. The joint work in North America and around the world indicates that cooperation is possible, even desirable. Local churches of different communions could find a new source of identity, a new sense of purpose by joining in mission study.

Every idea for mission education in the local church suggested in this book could be accomplished jointly by two or more churches. Beyond learning and thinking together, joint mission education could enlarge minds and hearts to the reality of "one world in mission."

Here is a list of ways local churches can cooperate in mission education. Can you add to the list?

(1) Churches join in "hosting" a missionary or national speaker.

(2) Churches join in viewing and studying a mission film.

(3) Churches join in mission study programs.

(4) Churches join in holding a "Mission Festival."

(5) Churches share among each other mission publications and books.

(6) Pulpit exchange based on mission theme.

(7) Churches join in preparing a mission display for the community.

(8) Churches join, inviting the community's cooperation, in a clothing drive or other service project.

DOUBLE RESPONSE

A chain of events led one local midwest church to re-commitment to mission. An inner city pastor told them of renewal in an urban ghetto; a national from Taiwan, studying at the local college, visited one Sunday and witnessed to the meaning of Christ in his life; a businessman traveled to Sao Paulo, Brazil, and came in contact with a dynamic Christian fellowship there; the youth group spent a weekend working with a home for senior citizens; a young member away to college shared in an ecumenical Work Camp in Europe; the women of the church got a vision from a special study program on South Africa. New ideas, new information, new experiences, all interrelated to the life of the one local church led to a group sense of dedication to mission.

What should happen? Be content with inspiration, warm feelings? The church determined to "double their mission response." They took some very specific steps.

(1) They doubled the number of "mission books" in the congregational library. (Fourteen books were still not many, of course; the new seven represented high quality compared to cast-offs in the first seven.)

(2) Efforts were made to increase subscriptions to the denominational mission magazine. Subscribers rose from five to seventeen. And four individuals, along with the congregational library, started receiving, and reading, a mission magazine from another denomination.

(3) The church's budget was redesigned to carry 120 percent of their "load" for the conference. An additional 10 percent was designated for other mission projects.

(4) An overseas effort and/or person, along with a related or similar national effort and/or person, were included in the church's petitions each Sunday morning. Such prayers were also included in organizations' devotional periods.

(5) Each congregational organization redesigned its program format to include stronger focus on mission education resources. A goal was set for at least one meeting per year on a national mission project and one for an overseas effort. Leaders in the Sunday church school began collecting information and materials to be interwoven as illustrations into regular curricula.

(6) The editor of the parish newspaper starting placing a mission item in each issue of the monthly. Quotes and "fillers" were used in the Sunday bulletin. Letters from missionaries, quotations from books, pictures of interest were placed on the church bulletin board and in classrooms.

(7) The church deacons appointed a subcommittee on mission, relating it to the parish committee on "corporate life." The group of three persons was asked to keep the cause of mission before the congregation, utilizing the regular organization and program channels.

(8) The choir director began seeking out music from overseas, or items with special mission content, for both the adult and children choirs. Liturgies, litanies, prayers and other worship forms were gleaned from overseas and ecumenical sources and utilized in the local church worship.

WHAT CAN I DO?

The missionary speaker has sparked your imagination. Or, the sermon has stirred you toward action. The film has shown vividly the need of human beings in a specific situation. Where are the handles? What can you do?

All too often, both the mission speaker and the listener are content to be "inspired" and then move along. *A response is required.* Here are four aspects of a meaningful response to mission inspiration.

(1) *Be informed.* How frequently we do not even know where in the world our speaker comes from or has served! Can we distinguish between Nigeria, Liberia, Siberia and Algeria? Where are Guyana, New Guinea or Guinea? Examine a map, read a book, select the right TV program, converse with an overseas visitor. Learn about the world, about its problems. Be interested enough to be informed.

(2) *Pray.* The private "closet," the personal "prayer list," the intimate association through intercessory prayer is part of our response to mission. Prayer should be a natural and effective involvement in mission. The life of a local church should be permeated with "mission prayer."

(3) *Provide support.* Financial contributions are part of

our response. Every local church should be supporting *fully* its apportioned share in the mission budget of the denomination. The local church normally channels this major "mission support" through a regional jurisdiction, e.g., district, conference, synod, diocese. A good number of local churches do not support *fully* the total work of their denomination through this general apportionment or benevolence; but that is the major financial response to mission! After fulfilling this task, local churches and individuals can find additional channels; denominational opportunities and other worthy "causes" are available. "Your heart will always be where your riches are." (Matt. 6:21 TEV) Your bankbook or checkbook continues to reflect your values, to indicate your response to mission.

(4) *Evangelize.* You have become excited about the Gospel changing lives, making people new and whole. The story is not alone about these happenings in some faraway land (though, indeed, it occurs there, too), or in a state or province across the continent (though, indeed, it occurs there, too), or in a neighboring "mission situation." Mission begins with YOU: you are made new and whole, your life is changed, your values are readjusted. You become a *missionary,* charged to evangelize where you are. Mission response means being a missionary right here!

voices
in mission

Biographic notes are presented below for the authors quoted in this volume.

Beaver, R. Pierce—Retired professor of history of missions, University of Chicago Divinity School.

Bouman, Pieter—Former staff member of the World Council of Churches, related to Young World Program of the Freedom from Hunger Campaign. Citizen of Holland.

Bridston, Keith R.—Professor of theology and mission at the Pacific Lutheran Theological Seminary, Berkeley, California.

Camara, Dom Helder—Roman Catholic archbishop of Recife, Brazil.

Casteren, Inga-Brita—Staff member, Commission on World Mission and Evangelism, World Council of Churches, Geneva.

Castro, Emilio—Director of the Commission on World Mission and Evangelism, World Council of Churches, Geneva. Citizen of Uruguay.

Dietterich, Paul M.—Staff member of the Center for Parish Development, Naperville, Illinois.

Eastman, A. Theodore—Rector of St. Alban's Episcopal Church, Washington, D.C.

Ellzey, Charles H.—Staff member of the Center for Parish Development, Naperville, Illinois.

Johnson, E. H.—Staff member of the Board of World Missions, Presbyterian Church in Canada.

May, Edward C.—Director of the Office for World Community, Lutheran Council in the United States of America, New York.

Neill, Stephen—Former bishop in the Church of South India and Associate General Secretary of the World Council of Churches, currently heads department of philosophy and religious studies at University College, Nairobi, Kenya.

Niles, D. T.—Deceased noted evangelist. Former General Secretary, East Asia Christian Conference. Methodist. Citizen of Sri Lanka.

Pagura, Federico—Pastor of the Central Church of Mendoza (Cuyana Region), Superintendent of the Cuyana Region, Mendoza, Argentina.

Ranck, J. Allan—Former director of the Department of Education for Mission, National Council of Churches.

Scherer, James A.—Professor of missions, Lutheran School of Theology at Chicago.

Smith, Eugene L.—Minister of United Methodist Church, Denville, New Jersey. Former executive secretary of the U.S. Committee for the World Council of Churches.

Sovik, Arne—Staff member of the Department of Studies, Lutheran World Federation, Geneva. Citizen of the United States.

Taylor, John V.—General secretary of the Church Missionary Society, London. Citizen of England.

Trexler, Edgar R.—Associate editor, *The Lutheran,* magazine of the Lutheran Church in America, Philadelphia.

Trueblood, Elton—Professor at Large, Earlham College, Richmond, Indiana.

Vikner, David L.—Executive director, Division for World Mission and Ecumenism, Lutheran Church in America, New York.

Webster, Douglas—Professor of mission, Selly Oak Colleges, Birmingham. Citizen of England.

Wedel, Cynthia—Associate director of the Center for a Voluntary Society, Washington, D.C. Former president of the National Council of Churches in the U.S.A.

notes

1. A. Theodore Eastman, *Missions: "In" or Out?* (New York: Friendship Press, 1967), pp. 21-22.
2. Elton Trueblood, *The Validity of the Christian Mission* (New York: Harper and Row, 1972), pp. 92-93.
3. R. Pierce Beaver, *From Missions to Mission* (New York: Association Press, 1964), pp. 61-62.
4. Emilio Castro, From notes of an address on October 29, 1972 to the United Methodist Board of Global Ministries.
5. Edward C. May, From an unpublished manuscript.
6. Federico Pagura, Excerpt from an article appearing in *World Update: Latin America* (New York: Friendship Press, 1973).
7. Douglas Webster, *Unchanging Mission* (London: Hodder and Stoughton, 1965), pp. 19-20.
8. Cynthia Wedel, *Faith or Fear and Future Shock* (New York: Friendship Press, 1974), pp. 27-28.
9. D. T. Niles, *The Message and Its Messengers* (Nashville: Abingdon Press, 1966), pp. 50-51.
10. John V. Taylor, *For All The World* (Philadelphia: Westminster Press, 1967), pp. 68-70.
11. Keith R. Bridston, *Mission Myth and Reality* (New York: Friendship Press, 1965), pp. 39-40.
12. Arne Sovik, *Salvation Today* (Minneapolis: Augsburg, 1973), pp. 45-48, 50-51, 53, 56.
13. Pieter M. Bouman, *Can the World Share the Wealth?* (New York: Friendship Press, 1969), pp. 6-7.
14. Eastman, *Missions: "In" or Out?*, pp. 9, 11-12.
15. Trueblood, *Validity of the Christian Mission*, pp. 56-57.
16. Eastman, *Missions: "In" or Out?*, pp. 25-26.
17. World Division, United Methodist Board of Global Ministries.
18. David L. Vikner, From a press release of the News Bureau of the Lutheran Church in America, November 13, 1973.

19. Stephen Neill, *Call to Mission* (Philadelphia: Fortress Press, 1970), pp. 95-96.
20. John V. Taylor, *The Go-Between God* (Philadelphia: Fortress Press, 1973), p. 38.
21. Bridston, *Mission Myth and Reality,* pp. 98-100.
22. Edgar R. Trexler, *The New Face of Missions* (St. Louis: Concordia Publishing House, 1973), pp. 55-56.
23. Eugene L. Smith, *Mandate for Mission* (New York: Friendship Press, 1968), pp. 25-28.
24. Dom Helder Camara, Excerpt from an interview appearing in *World Update: Latin America* (New York: Friendship Press, 1972).
25. Douglas Webster, *Yes to Mission* (London: SCM Press, 1966), pp. 23-24.
26. James A. Scherer, *Global Living Here and Now* (New York: Friendship Press, 1974), pp. 97-98.
27. Trueblood, *Validity of the Christian Mission,* p. 109.
28. E. H. Johnson, *For a Time Like This* (New York: Friendship Press, 1973), excerpted from pp. 109, 110, 111-112.
29. Webster, *Unchanging Mission,* pp. 55-56, 59.
30. Johnson, *For a Time Like This,* pp. 117-118.
31. Inga-Brita Casteren, "Education for Missions," *International Review of Mission,* Vol. LXII, No. 245, January 1973, pp. 94-95.
32. J. Allan Ranck, *Education for Mission* (New York: Friendship Press, 1961), pp. 50-52, 56-58.
33. Ranck, *Education for Mission,* pp. 44-46.
34. Charles H. Ellzey and Paul M. Dietterich, *The Center Letter* (Naperville, Illinois, April 1973), Vol. 3, No. 4.
35. Taylor, *For All the World,* pp. 74-76.
36. From *Today's English Version of the New Testament,* American Bible Society, 1966, 1971.
37. Martin Luther, *The Small Catechism in Contemporary English* (Philadelphia: Fortress Press, 1960), p. 12.
38. From *The Interpreter,* United Methodist Church publication, November-December 1973, pp. 26-27.